STUDIES IN GERMAN COLONIAL HISTORY

T0347957

Other books by W. O. Henderson

The Lancashire Cotton Famine (Manchester University Press, 1934)
Britain and Industrial Europe (Liverpool University Press, 1954)
The State and the Industrial Revolution in Prussia (Liverpool University Press, 1958)
The Zollverein (second edition: Frank Cass and Company, 1959)
The Industrial Revolution on the Continent (Frank Cass and Company, 1961)

STUDIES IN GERMAN
COLONIAL HISTORY

W. O. HENDERSON

Routledge
Taylor & Francis Group

LONDON AND NEW YORK

First published 1962 by
FRANK CASS AND COMPANY LIMITED

Published 2006 by Routledge
2 Park Square, Milton Park, Abingdon, Oxfordshire OX14 4RN
711 Third Avenue, New York, NY 10017

First issued in paperback 2014

Routledge is an imprint of the Taylor and Francis Group, an informa business

Copyright © 1962 W. O. Henderson

Second impression 1976

ISBN 13: 978-0-7146-1674-2 (hbk)
ISBN 13: 978-0-415-76069-0 (pbk)

ACKNOWLEDGEMENT

The author desires to thank the editors of *History*, the *Economic History Review*, *German Life and Letters*, and the *Scottish Geographical Magazine* for permission to reprint articles which have appeared in those journals. The chapter on the role of the chartered companies in the development of Germany's overseas possessions was delivered as a paper to a seminar at the Institute of Commonwealth Studies of the University of London and is now published for the first time. My thanks are due to my colleague, Mr. D. A. Farnie, who has helped me to correct the proofs of this book.

W.O.H.

CONTENTS

INTRODUCTION TO SECOND IMPRESSION

SINCE these essays appeared in 1962 several books and articles on various aspects of the history of the German colonial empire have been published. Marxist historians are just as critical today of Germany's colonial administration as their fathers were before 1914. In the German Democratic Republic historians have delved into the archives of the Colonial Office to unearth documents which would appear to discredit Germany's colonial record. Manfred Nussbaum, for example, in his study of the colonial policies of Bismarck, Caprivi, and Hohenlohe (*Vom 'Kolonialentusiasmus' zur Kolonial-politik der Monopole*, 1962) exaggerates the influence of a few entrepreneurs and bankers, such as Woermann and Hansemann, on Bismarck's colonial policy. He does so in the hope of showing that Lenin's doctrine that imperialism represents the highest form of capitalism is confirmed by the history of Germany's overseas possessions. Similarly the contributors to *Kamerun unter deutscher Kolonialherrschaft* (edited by H. Stoecker, 1968) assiduously collect evidence to denounce German rule in the Cameroons and make no attempt to give an unbiassed account of the administration of the colony between 1884 and 1914. On the other hand students are indebted to various scholars whose researches have deepened our knowledge of the history of Germany's overseas territories. For example John Iliffe's excellent monograph of *Tanganyika under German Rule, 1905–12* (1969) and O. F. Raum's chapter on changes in tribal life under German administration in East Africa in the *History of East Africa*, Vol. II, 1965, are examples of well balanced and unbiassed surveys of one of Germany's most important colonies in Africa.

1976   W. O. H.

INTRODUCTION

THE study of Germany as a Colonial Power can be undertaken from a number of different points of view. The acquisition of overseas possessions by the Reich was an important aspect of Bismarck's work and no examination of his policy would be complete without considering his achievements in the field of colonial expansion. The establishment of German authority in the interior of the overseas territories, the setting up of organs of administration, the 'colonial scandals', and the 'new era' of colonial policy in which Dr. Dernburg played a leading role are a significant aspect of German history in the reign of Wilhelm II. The desire of the Pan-Germans to expand their overseas empire at the expense of other countries (such as Portugal) and the economic penetration of the Ottoman Empire (the Berlin-Baghdad railway project) contributed to bringing about that distrust of Germany which was a factor in causing the arms race in the early twentieth century. The campaigns which led to the conquest of the German colonies were no mere 'sideshows' for they contributed to the defeat of the Reich in the first World War.

Examined from these points of view the rise and fall of the German colonial empire may be regarded as one aspect of the foreign and imperial policies of Bismarck's Reich. The overseas possessions were also significant in Germany's domestic affairs. On the one hand the colonies were a unifying factor in the new Reich since they were —like Alsace and Lorraine—truly 'national' territories which were a part of the Empire and did not belong to any one of the Federal States into which Germany was divided. On the other hand the colonies were a cause of internal strife in Germany. The political parties were sharply divided on questions concerning colonial policy and the future of the overseas possessions was a vital issue in the hotly contested Reichstag general election of 1907.

Again, it is possible to view the German colonial empire from an African or from a Pacific angle rather than from a European point of view. An examination of such aspects of Germany's work in her colonies as exploration, missionary activities, land policy, plantations, railways, and native welfare shows the profound effect of the German impact upon Africa, Shantung and the Pacific islands.

No European country has held overseas possessions for so short a period as Germany. The colonial empire began in 1884 when Bismarck placed under imperial protections the establishments set up by Lüderitz at Angra Pequeña. It ended in 1919 when the Treaty of Versailles deprived Germany of all her colonies. A number of those who had helped to found the overseas empire were still alive when Germany's career as a Colonial Power came to an abrupt end. This fact to some extent simplifies the task of the historian. Germans have been prolific writers on various aspects of colonial affairs but there are limits as to what can be said about an empire which lasted only thirty-five years. Students of German colonial history have less material to deal with than scholars who are interested in the development of British, French, Dutch or Spanish expansion overseas.

Moreover the history of German colonization, though it covers only a short period of time, is particularly interesting because German colonial policy quickly passed through several significant phases. Changes which in the overseas possessions of other countries were a matter of gradual evolution took place much more rapidly in the German colonial empire. The Germans were late-comers in the field of colonial expansion and it is not surprising that they made mistakes at first. But they learned quickly. Between 1884 and 1914 German colonial policy passed rapidly through several distinct phases.

The first six years (1884-90), when Bismarck was Chancellor, saw the establishment of the colonial empire and the attempt to administer it through chartered companies. This method of colonial government failed and the Reich had to shoulder the full responsibility for the administration of the colonial empire.

The second sixteen years in the history of Germany as a Colonial Power—between Bismarck's fall in 1890 and the crisis caused by the 'colonial scandals' in 1906—saw the establishment of the authority of the Reich in most of the interior of the overseas possessions. It was an era of 'little wars' against the natives. But it was a period that ended in disaster and disillusionment. There were serious revolts both in South West Africa and in East Africa and grave scandals in colonial administration were brought to light. The economic results of colonization were disappointing. Bitter controversies on the colonial question heralded a 'new era' in the administration of the overseas territories. Between 1907 and 1914 a more enlightened policy was pursued and by the eve of the first World War there was much less to criticize in Germany's colonial rule than there had been only a few years before. Administrators such as Dernburg, Rechenberg, Solf and Schnee were men of ability, courage and integrity. The loyalty of the natives to the Germans during the colonial campaigns of the first World War suggests that there was no longer any serious discontent with German rule.

The study of Germany's colonial empire is, however, beset with certain difficulties. Few historical events can have bequeathed to posterity such a legacy of controversial literature. There were sharp differences of opinion in Germany itself about the acquisition and the administration of the overseas possessions. And there were controversies between foreigners who denounced the colonial record of the Reich and Germans who defended it. Even before the German flag had been hoisted over a single overseas territory there were lively arguments concerning the desirability of founding an overseas empire. In the 1870's some German writers took the view that it would be a mistake for the Reich to enter the ranks of the Colonial Powers. They considered that overseas possessions cost men and money to acquire and would be a constant burden on the taxpayer. Bismarck to the end of his life doubted the wisdom of acquiring colonies. He believed that it was a great advantage to Germany to be a purely Continental state with no overseas commitments. He saw that the establishment of an overseas empire might involve Germany in serious disputes with Britain upon whose neutrality in Continental conflicts he had hitherto been able to rely. But there were early 'colonial enthusiasts' who demanded the establishment of an overseas empire so that Germany might control much needed raw materials and foodstuffs and might find new outlets for her manufactured goods. The desirability of settling Germans under their own flag—instead of allowing them to emigrate to the United States—was another argument in favour of founding colonies.

When Bismarck established German colonies in the 1880's the controversy took a new turn. Many of those who had once criticized the founding of territories overseas now became critics of the newly established colonial administrations. Every blunder in the handling of the natives and every failure of a colonial company enabled the critics to say that their worst fears had proved to be correct.

This controversy reached its climax in the early years of the twentieth century when Socialists and Catholics joined to denounce those responsible for 'colonial scandals'. Erzberger claimed that millions of marks had been squandered in the overseas territories while officials and planters were accused of gross cruelty to the natives. Eventually the government was unable to resist the demand that the courts should determine the truth of charges of this kind. The trial of Carl Peters and his dismissal from the colonial service showed that even the popular founder of German East Africa could be brought to book for his misdeeds. The revolt of the Herero in South West Africa and the Majimaji rising in German East Africa showed that the Germans had failed to establish themselves firmly in two of their most important overseas territories.

In 1907, however, a 'new era' dawned in the German colonies. Dr. Dernburg, the first Colonial Minister, made strenuous efforts to reform the administration of the colonial empire. But the controversies continued. On the one hand Dernburg's right-wing critics denounced the reformers as men who were ruining the colonies by slackening the strict discipline which was necessary to maintain order among the natives. On the other hand the Socialists eagerly watched for any sign of a lapse into the old discredited methods of colonial administration.

During the first World War a new controversy arose. In order to blacken Germany's name in neutral countries English publicists (such as Northcliffe) and eventually the British Government embarked upon a campaign to brand the Germans as inhuman monsters who had maltreated the natives in their colonies in the vilest fashion. Some of the evidence assembled to support these allegations was derived from criticisms made by Germans themselves of the colonial administration of the Reich particularly before the 'new era' of 1907-14. But some of the allegations concerning Germany's colonial record which were made at this time were either sheer inventions or were garbled versions of accusations which had long before been shown to have little foundation in fact.

When Germany had to surrender her colonies in 1919 the Allies explained that they were not doing anything so vulgar as to annex somebody else's territories. Such an action would be contrary to the letter and to the spirit of Wilson's fourteen points. They claimed that they were acting from the highest motives and that they were rescuing millions of down-trodden natives from a cruel and despotic rule. The Germans denounced what they called the 'colonial guilt lie'. They admitted that unfortunate mistakes had been made in the early days of colonization but they claimed that the worst abuses had been eradicated long before 1914. They argued that all Colonial Powers had, at one time or another, been guilty of actions which they had later wished to forget. The 'red rubber' scandals in the Congo had not been forgotten and the Germans claimed that it was pure impudence on the part of the French, the Belgians, and the Portuguese to set themselves up as judges of German colonial administration. The controversy continued throughout the twenty years between the two World Wars and when Hitler came into power he demanded the return to Germany of her former overseas possessions.

In view of all these controversies the historian of the German colonies has to scrutinize with the greatest care any document, book, pamphlet, article or report that he believes may contain information of value. Much of what has been written on Germany's overseas possessions is tainted by propaganda. The difficulties that bar the way to the discovery of what really happened in the German colonies between 1884 and 1914 are a challenge to the historian. It is of importance that the grain should be sifted from the chaff and that the truth should be ascertained.

Chapter I

THE GERMAN COLONIAL EMPIRE

THE story of Germany's colonial empire has often been inadequately treated in general works on European history. The results of Germany's acquisition of territory overseas on her foreign policy are generally recognized, but the development of the colonies themselves is frequently neglected. Moreover, an impartial consideration of the question has been hampered by long and bitter controversies. The German colonial empire was conquered during the first World War and was partitioned by the Allies, who claimed that Germany had misgoverned her colonies and was unfit to retain them. Germany indignantly repudiated this accusation. The appearance, on the one hand, of books charging the German colonial administration with all kinds of abuses[1] and, on the other, of publications designed to show Germany's work overseas in the most favourable light possible[2] has not facilitated the task of the student. It is best to go back to the evidence of those who wrote before the first World War.

Although Germany held no colonies before 1884 her people lacked neither colonial traditions nor experience in exploration and settlement. In the Middle Ages traders and settlers extended German influence both by land and sea. They moved down the Danube valley and along the Baltic coast. The Hanseatic League established trading posts in Baltic and North Sea ports. In the great Age of Discovery Germany was distracted by internal struggles and was not situated near the new trade routes of the world, so that she did not play an important part in exploration or trade in the East Indies or America. Her share in opening up new countries at this time was not, however, entirely insignificant. Thus in the first half of the sixteenth century the Welsers, a German banking house, governed part of Venezuela for some thirty years, and Federmann, one of the settlers, explored Colombia. In the seventeenth century, Branden-burg-Prussia secured a few possessions overseas. The Great Elector bought two trading stations on the south-east coast of India, and founded the African Commercial Company which established itself on the Gold Coast. His successor purchased part of the island of Tobago. Prussia, however, was not strong enough to develop a colonial empire, and these possessions were given up early in the eighteenth century.

1

The need for colonies began to be felt in Germany after 1815. Many Germans were emigrating owing to political discontent and to economic distress. Over a million Germans went to the United States of America between 1830 and 1860, most of them settling in the Old North-West—north of the Ohio and east of the Mississippi—and in Texas. Others went to the Province of Rio Grande do Sul in Brazil and to Valdivia in Chile. As the Germans settled under foreign flags they were often lost to their native country. The establishment of a colonial empire in temperate regions would enable settlers to retain their nationality and culture and would increase Germany's importance as a World Power. Unfortunately most of the temperate regions suitable for white settlement had already been secured by other Powers. In America, expansion was barred by the Monroe Doctrine. Further, as Germany became industrialized, it was felt that she should secure control over tropical regions which could supply her with raw materials and food in return for manufactured articles. There were still rich tropical areas in Africa and the Pacific which had not been annexed by European States. But owing to pressing problems at home, the lack of naval forces and the fear of antagonizing other Powers, neither individual German States nor the Germanic Confederation made any attempt to obtain territory overseas. Meantime explorers, missionaries and traders were laying the foundations of future colonial expansion.

Of the work of German explorers in the nineteenth century, much of which was done for foreign governments and associations, only a few outstanding examples can be mentioned here. In Africa, Barth carefully examined Lake Chad and neighbouring regions in the early fifties. Von der Decken surveyed the southern slopes of Mount Kilimanjaro in 1861-62. Schweinfurth's expedition of 1868-72 investigated the upper Nile. At the same time Nachtigal was exploring the River Shari which runs into Lake Chad. Between 1879 and 1886 Junker travelled in the region between this lake and the Nile. Von Wissmann twice crossed central Africa in the eighties. In South America, Alexander von Humboldt made an important journey to Venezuela, Peru and Mexico at the beginning of the century. Some twenty years later von Spix and von Martius were sent by the King of Bavaria to South America and they explored the River Amazon. Valuable information of the physical features of China was secured by von Richtofen in seven expeditions undertaken between 1868 and 1872. In Australia, Leichhardt crossed Queensland from Sydney to the Gulf of Carpentaria in the forties and (wrote Lang) 'virtually added a vast and valuable province to the British Empire'. In New Zealand, von Hochstetter and von Haast undertook a geological survey of Auckland Province in 1858. Von Haast also travelled in Nelson Province. German missionaries, too, were active in many parts of the world, particularly in Africa. The Barmen Rhine Mission, for example, worked in Namaqualand, and the Basel Mission—a Swiss body run by Germans—worked in Togoland.

The development of her commerce and shipping was another factor in the extension of German influence overseas. Recovery from the paralysis produced by Napoleon's Continental System was slow. Germany's sea-borne trade was, to a great extent, in the hands of the English and Dutch. The petty rivalries of the German coastal States, the stringent navigation laws and the differential harbour dues of her rivals hampered the development of a mercantile marine. The lack of a fleet was felt particularly in the Mediterranean, where the activities of the Barbary pirates menaced commerce. In the thirties and forties the Prussian mercantile marine expanded with the revival of the Baltic corn trade. More important was the rise of the shipping of Hamburg and Bremen in the great Atlantic trades. Between twenty and thirty German vessels were bringing sugar and coffee from Brazil in the early thirties. Hamburg's prosperity was temporarily checked by the disastrous fire of May 1842. The founding of the Hamburg-America Company in 1847 and of the North German Lloyd (Bremen) ten years later mark the beginning of a new era of prosperity for the Hanse Towns. The activities of three great Hamburg companies in regions which subsequently became German colonies deserve mention. The firm of O'Swald controlled much of the trade of the east coast of Africa in the sixties, Woermann held a powerful position on the Cameroons coast in West Africa, and the house of Godeffroy virtually monopolized the trade of Samoa.

The establishment of the North German Confederation in 1867, and its expansion into the German Empire four years later, led to a new interest in the acquisition of territory overseas. Colonial enthusiasts claimed that a Great Power which aspired to play a leading part in world affairs should have possessions abroad. They considered that Germany needed homes for emigrants, fresh sources of raw materials and tropical foods, new markets for manufactured articles. The vast bulk of the nation, however, felt that to acquire colonies might be costly in men and money and might lead to serious disputes with other Powers. It would above all be foolish to quarrel with Britain at a time when Germany was anxious to keep France completely isolated. Bismarck declared that 'for Germany to acquire colonies would be like a poverty-stricken Polish nobleman providing himself with silks and sables when he needed shirts.' Gradually, however, the importunities of traders, financiers and others interested in expansion overseas began to have their effect upon the Chancellor. In 1876 a group of merchants suggested to him the establishment of a protectorate over the Transvaal. Bismarck had rejected such a proposal before and he rejected it again. But on this occasion he admitted that Germany could not dispense permanently with colonies. The foreign situation was not favourable for any action at the moment.

Between 1876 and 1884 Bismarck frequently stated that he did not wish to acquire colonies, and there seems no reason to doubt his sincerity. But he felt that Germany's prestige as a Great Power must be maintained, and consequently he supported Germans abroad in their disputes with foreign countries. He also concluded commercial treaties with native rulers in the Pacific. When the house of Godeffroy failed in 1878 he endeavoured to maintain Germany's position in the Samoan Islands by submitting a Bill to the Reichstag for the underwriting of a new company to take over Godeffroy's rights from their creditors, the London firm of Baring Brothers. The National Liberals, whose support Bismarck still needed, rejected the proposal, and Bismarck recognized that the time was not yet ripe for the founding of colonies.

In the early eighties German expansionists could point to renewed colonial activity by foreign countries. England's purchase of some of the Suez Canal shares in 1875 and her bombardment of the forts of Alexandria in July 1882 were the prelude to intervention in Egypt. At the same time she was active in East Africa, West Africa and New Guinea. The French virtually established a protectorate over Tunis in 1881 and the Italians were taking the first steps towards the foundation of colonies on the shores of the Red Sea. Clearly if Germany did not act promptly the few remaining regions of the world suitable for exploitation would be appropriated by other Powers.

German public opinion was becoming more favourable to the establishment of colonies. The rise of economic nationalism may be seen in the adoption of a policy of Protection in 1879. The old arguments on the need for raw materials and new markets, which were put forward by Fabri in his *Does Germany need Colonies?*, appeared to have a greater force. Moreover, the new wave of emigration which followed the industrial depression of the seventies caused some alarm. The support given to two societies formed in the early eighties to foster colonization indicates the new interest in the question. The *Kolonialverein* (Colonial Society) was founded in 1882 and had over ten thousand members within three years. Carl

Peters' *Gesellschaft für deutsche Kolonisation* (Society for German Colonization) of 1884 hoped to raise money to finance colonial enterprise in East Africa. Rivalry between these two bodies ended in their amalgamation in 1887 when the *Deutsche Kolonialgesellschaft* (German Colonial Society) was set up.

In 1884, Bismarck was ready to act. The conclusion of the Dual Alliance (Germany and Austria-Hungary, 1879), the League of the three Emperors (Germany, Austria-Hungary and Russia, 1881) and the Triple Alliance (Germany, Austria-Hungary and Italy, 1882) initiated a brief period of diplomatic calm before the storms caused principally by Boulangism and the Bulgarian question of 1885-87. Bismarck felt able to face British opposition in colonial affairs. Early in 1883 he asked what claims Britain had to territories in the Angra Pequeña district in South West Africa. Britain answered that she held Walfish Bay and the Guano Islands and that her rights would be infringed by any claims to lands between Cape Colony and Angola. Bismarck thereupon inquired on what grounds Britain took up this attitude. No reply was forthcoming. On 24 April, 1884, Bismarck placed under Imperial protection the 'establishments' of the German merchant Lüderitz at Angra Pequeña (Lüderitz Bay).

This was followed by the founding of a German colonial empire in Africa and the Pacific. Some features of this expansion overseas deserve notice. It was accomplished in the astonishingly short period of six years. Few new acquisitions were made after 1890. It was marked by sharp practice on the part of adventurers who went to Africa ostensibly as traders or explorers and then suddenly produced authority from the Government to conclude treaties with native chiefs for placing their territories under German protection. On the other hand it is remarkable that, although there were serious disputes, particularly with Britain, the acquisition of colonies did not involve Germany in war with any European Power. Further, except for von Wissmann's suppression of the Arab revolt in East Africa, there were no military expeditions against the natives in the German colonies in the eighties. This is in strong contrast with the difficulties that other European countries were having in Africa at this time. Another feature worthy of notice is the attempt to govern some of the colonies by chartered companies. Bismarck desired to reduce to a minimum the responsibilities of the home government.

The German colonial empire eventually had an area of a million square miles and an estimated native population of about fifteen millions. Most of the colonies were in Africa. The largest and most promising was German East Africa (Tanganyika) with an area of 384,000 square miles. Valuable tropical products such as cotton,

5

rubber, tobacco and coffee could be raised. Some of the highlands were suitable for white settlement. There were adequate ports. The first task of the Germans was to break the power of the Arab slave traders and this was done in 1888. Carl Peters, who had done so much to stake out Germany's claims to this region, was bitterly disappointed at the Anglo-German Treaty of 1890 by which Germany recognized Britain's rights over Witu, Uganda, Nyasaland and Zanzibar in return for Heligoland. He complained that 'two kingdoms, Witu and Uganda, had been sacrificed for a bath-tub in the North Sea.' On the west coast of Africa Germany secured three colonies—South West Africa (322,450 square miles), the Cameroons (Old Cameroons 192,000 square miles, New Cameroons 100,000 square miles) and Togoland (33,000 square miles). South West Africa included much desert, but diamonds were found in 1908 and some districts were suitable for white settlement. Many difficulties had to be overcome before the country could be developed. Expensive public works had to be constructed and native hostility had to be overcome. The Cameroons and Togoland were useful sources of tropical products, but their climate was unsuitable for white settlement.

In the Pacific, Germany obtained the north-east of the island of New Guinea (Kaiser Wilhelmsland), some of the Solomon Islands, New Britain (Neu Pommern), New Ireland (Neu Mecklenburg), the Duke of York Islands (Neu Lauenburg) and some smaller islands. These islands produced copra, phosphates, rubber, coffee and so forth. They were regarded as useful for the construction of naval and trading harbours, coaling and cable stations.

Regarded as a whole, the German possessions overseas had two sources of weakness. First, the colonial empire was a series of scattered territories that had been seized because they were the only areas available. It had no geographical unity such as that possessed by the empires of Britain and France. The British Empire was linked by the great sea routes of the North Atlantic and the Indian Ocean. An important part of the French Empire could be regarded as a natural expansion of the mother country across the Mediterranean. Secondly, the German possessions lacked some of their natural harbours and were difficult to defend. Thus the chief port of German South West Africa (Walfish Bay) was in British hands. Similarly, Britain held the strategically important islands of Zanzibar and Pemba off the coast of German East Africa. The development of New Guinea was jealously watched by Australia.

Three periods may be distinguished in the development of Germany's colonial administration. The first was between 1884 and

6

1890, the period of Bismarck's acquisition of overseas possessions and of government by chartered companies. The second was from Bismarck's fall to 1906, a period of Imperial control. Serious mistakes were made and abuses led to native risings. The leading figure in this period was Dr. Kayser, the director of the colonial section of the Foreign Office in the early nineties. The third period was from 1906 to 1914, an era of colonial reform and economic progress associated with the name of Dr. Dernburg, who was in charge of the newly established Colonial Office.

Although there had been much expansionist propaganda Bismarck had to deal with serious opposition to his colonial policy. The Social Democrats argued that the seizure of colonies might benefit capitalists, but would lead to the exploitation of natives. The Radicals held that most of the colonies were useless for emigration, that their exploitation would be expensive and that tropical products could be obtained from the colonies of other countries. Critics were able to point to abuses. It was soon seen that most of the chartered companies were not governing the colonies properly. They were interested in securing quick profits and not in tackling problems of administration. The German South West Africa Company gave up its political rights in 1888, the German East Africa Company in 1891, the New Guinea Company in 1899. They survived as purely commercial concerns. In the Cameroons and Togoland there were no chartered companies.

After 1891, the principal German colonies were ruled by Governors responsible to the Emperor. In Berlin, colonial affairs were in the hands of the Colonial Section of the Foreign Office. There was also an advisory Colonial Council appointed by the Chancellor. Dr. Kayser, who was director of the department from 1890 to 1896, was only partially successful in dealing with the difficulties he had to face. He made two serious mistakes. First, unduly large concessions were made to companies. Thus nearly a third of German South West Africa was controlled by nine companies in 1903. Secondly, colonial administration was too centralized and bureaucratic and was in the hands of unsuitable persons—for example, army officers with no experience of tropical countries and their inhabitants. Misgovernment led to native risings, which had to be suppressed by costly military expeditions. The Social Democrats kept the question of colonial scandals before the Reichstag and some action was taken against the worst offenders. Thus Carl Peters, Leist (Governor of the Cameroons), Wehland (a judge in the Cameroons) and von Horn (Governor of Togoland) had to leave the colonial service. There was, however, a brighter side to German

7

colonial administration in the troubled years 1890-1906. Much exploration was undertaken. Some economic progress was made. Public works were constructed. A certain interest was taken in the welfare of natives. Mission schools and hospitals were set up. Valuable scientific work was done, particularly in the study of tropical medicine and tropical agriculture.

Opportunities for extending Germany's colonial empire were scanty between 1890 and 1896. The young Emperor Wilhelm II, who wanted Germany to have a place in the sun, cast envious eyes upon the vast African possessions of Belgium and Portugal and hoped to benefit from the weakness of Spain, Turkey and China to secure new territories and spheres of influence. In 1898 Germany obtained a naval base at Kiao Chow and in the same year the Spanish-American war enabled her to put pressure upon Spain to give up some of her islands in the Pacific. Eventually she bought three groups of islands—the Carolines, the Pelews and the Mariannes (except Guam). The Samoan Islands, which had been jointly governed by Britain, Germany and the United States for twenty years, were divided between these Powers in 1899. Germany obtained Opolu and Sawai. The Anglo-German Treaty of 1898 delimited spheres of influence in the Portuguese colonies in Africa in the event of Portugal obtaining a loan from these Powers on the security of her colonial customs receipts. Germany hoped for a speedy partition of the Portuguese colonies, but Britain did not. In 1899 Britain virtually destroyed the Treaty of 1898 by making an agreement with Portugal for the mutual protection of colonies. The Portuguese colonies never came on to the market. The Kaiser's hopes for establishing a protectorate over the Transvaal were also disappointed. In the Near East, however, he was more successful. Germany pursued a policy of 'peaceful penetration' in Turkey in the eighties and nineties, and in 1903 she secured the concession to build the Baghdad Railway.

Criticism of abuses in Germany's colonial administration came to a head in 1906. Loss of lands, forced labour and harsh punishments had driven the natives to revolt in the three principal African colonies. Von Puttkamer's inhuman treatment of natives in the Cameroons and General Trotha's savage suppression of the Herero revolt in South West Africa in 1905-6, were the culmination of years of misgovernment on the part of some of the colonial officials. Public opinion in Germany was aroused, and in 1906 the Reichstag rejected a supplementary colonial estimate. A general election followed and von Bülow triumphed over his Social Democrat and Centre (Roman-Catholic) opponents. But the Government had had a lesson and thorough reforms of the colonial administration were undertaken. The colonial section of the Foreign Office was raised to an independent Department in 1907. Dr. Dernburg was appointed Colonial Secretary and remained in office until 1910. He went to London and to Africa to see how Britain administered her colonies, and then visited the United States to study methods of cotton culture. Careful attention was paid to the training of officials, and a Colonial Institute was set up at Hamburg for this purpose. In the colonies German settlers and even some of the natives received a limited share in the management of local affairs. The colonial land policy was changed, and the Government tried to buy land back from the companies. Public works were pushed forward. The important railway from Dar-es-Salaam across East Africa to Kigoma, for example, was opened in 1914. Serious attention was paid to native welfare. Plans were made for the gradual abolition of domestic slavery. Compulsory labour might be used only on public works and it had to be paid for. None but officials might legally have a native flogged. Important research in tropical medicine was undertaken. Dr. Koch, who worked in East Africa, discovered a remedy for sleeping sickness. The new colonial policy had been in force for only seven years when the first World War broke out. Even in this short period some of its beneficent results were seen. The natives appeared to be reasonably contented. There were no risings and, on the whole, the natives were faithful to Germany during the first World War.

The Kaiser was as anxious as ever to extend Germany's territory overseas, but the opposition of Britain, France and Russia made this difficult. In 1911 Germany obtained a strip of French Equatorial Africa (the New Cameroons) in return for giving up all claims to Morocco. A year later a new Anglo-German agreement on the possible partition of the Portuguese colonies in Africa was reached. A different cause for intervention was envisaged this time. If the lives, property or vital interests of British or German citizens were threatened by disturbances in Mozambique or Angola and the Portuguese Government could not adequately protect them the two Powers would co-operate to safeguard their interests. The Baghdad Railway project was held up by the Young Turk revolution (1908) and by opposition from Britain, Russia and France. In June 1914 an Anglo-German agreement was initialled but it was never signed. By the outbreak of war the line had been built from Scutari across Anatolia to Adana (near Tarsus).

In some respects Germany was disappointed with her colonies. They attracted few settlers and they supplied German industry with only a small part of the raw materials it needed. With the exception of Togoland they failed to become self-supporting. They involved Germany in serious disputes with foreign Powers. On the other hand in judging her colonial achievements it must be remembered that Germany had a colonial empire for only thirty years.

During the first World War all Germany's possessions overseas were conquered by the Allies. Most of them were overrun without difficulty. In East Africa, however, von Lettow Vorbeck made a long and gallant resistance against superior numbers. After the war the colonial empire was partitioned among the victors, the territories being held as mandates for the League of Nations. The mandatory Powers tried to assimilate the former German colonies to their own colonies as much as possible. Thus South West Africa was administered as an integral part of the Union of South Africa. It may be observed, too, that although Japan left the League of Nations she did not give up her mandated islands in the Pacific.

REFERENCES

1. For example, the Foreign Office Handbook on *Treatment of Natives in German Colonies* (1920).
2. For example, H. Schnee, *German Colonisation Past and Future* (1926).

Chapter II

CHARTERED COMPANIES IN THE GERMAN COLONIES

<small>BISMARCK'S VIEWS ON COLONIAL ADMINISTRATION[1]</small>

WHEN the German colonial empire was established in 1884 Bismarck repeatedly expressed the view that chartered companies should be responsible for the administration of newly acquired overseas possessions. He argued that while senior Prussian civil servants and non-commissioned officers in the army performed their duties admirably at home they did not have the experience which would enable them to undertake the entirely different task of governing native peoples in Africa or the Pacific. Bismarck believed that it was merchants from Hamburg and Bremen—with their long experience of trading in the Cameroons, at Zanzibar and in Samoa—who should be prepared to shoulder the responsibilities of colonial administration because they alone had the necessary knowledge of the territories in which protectorates were being established.

Bismarck declared that he was opposed to any adoption of French colonial methods which were, in his view, unsuited to German needs. The French system, according to Bismarck, consisted of taking possession of a piece of territory, subduing the natives, establishing first a military and then a civil administration and finally hoping that French traders and settlers would follow in the footsteps of the soldiers and the officials. Bismarck thought that this was putting the cart before the horse. In his opinion trade should not follow the flag. On the contrary the flag should follow trade and the traders themselves should administer the colonies.

Two explanations may be given to account for Bismarck's adoption of this point of view. In the first place Bismarck himself had never had any experience of colonial administration. He had to make use of the experience of others. The French system of colonization—or what he thought to be the French system—did not commend itself to Bismarck. But the British system of chartered companies seemed to Bismarck to be admirably suited to Germany's needs in the 1880's. Britain had had three centuries of colonial experience and Bismarck argued that what was good enough for Britain should be good enough for the Reich. In view of Bismarck's professed admiration for British colonial methods it is a little surprising that in practice he did not devise colonial charters on the British model. The charter given to the German Colonial Society in respect of territories in East Africa bore very little resemblance to any charter granted to a British company.

The second reason why Bismarck favoured chartered companies concerned the financial aspect of colonization. After 1871 the national finances of the Reich were based upon the principle that indirect taxes were levied by the Federal Government while direct taxes were levied by the individual States. Federal budget deficits were covered by grants from the individual States. Bismarck desired that the Federal Exchequer should be as self-supporting as possible and should not rely any more than was absolutely necessary upon the contributions of the separate States. This was one reason why Bismarck adopted a fiscal policy of Protection since additional revenues from customs duties would increase the funds under the direct control of the central Government. Unfortunately the Government's expenditure was increasing owing to the rising cost of the army and the social services. Bismarck viewed with misgivings the possibility of incurring heavy expenditure in the establishment and maintenance of a colonial empire. In the circumstances it is not surprising that he should argue in favour of a system of colonial administration which would throw virtually the entire cost upon the shareholders of privileged chartered companies.

Unfortunately the merchants engaged in colonial trade were not prepared to accept the role that Bismarck had designed for them. The great German trading houses operating at Zanzibar and on the west coast of Africa refused to have anything to do with Bismarck's schemes for the establishment of chartered companies with sovereign rights. No companies enjoying sovereign powers were ever set up in the Cameroons, Togoland or South West Africa.[2] It was only with considerable difficulty that a company was induced to accept sovereign powers in New Guinea and that the Jaluit Company was persuaded to pay the costs of administration in the Marshall Islands. In East Africa a charter was originally given not to a trading company but to a penniless private society. This was no auspicious inauguration of a policy of colonial government by chartered companies.

GERMAN EAST AFRICA COMPANY, 1884-1890[3]

Germany's colony in East Africa was founded in 1884 as the result of an expedition led by Carl Peters which was sent out by the Society for German Colonization. This association had been founded in Berlin in March 1884 by Carl Peters and by Count Felix Behr-Bandelin who was an influential Pomeranian landlord and an official at Court. The society's executive committee, at its first meeting, defined its object as 'the founding of German plantation and commercial colonies by securing adequate capital for colonization, by finding and securing possession of regions suitable for colonization, and by attracting German immigrants to those regions.' The resources of the society were insufficient to fit out an expedition as its only income was that derived from members' annual subscriptions of five marks. But 75,000 marks were quickly raised by offering to the public shares of 5,000, 500 and 50 marks. Shareholders were entitled to land in the colony that it was proposed to establish.

In the autumn of 1884 Carl Peters, Karl Ludwig Jühlke and Count Joachim von Pfeil—three young adventurers all under thirty years of age—went to Zanzibar accompanied by a gentleman named Otto. Here the German consul showed Peters a communication from the German Foreign Office which stated that he could expect from the Government 'neither Imperial protection nor any guarantees for his personal safety'. Nevertheless the expedition went to the mainland and followed the River Wami into the interior. By a dozen treaties signed with native chiefs whose territory lay in Usagara, Useguha, Nguru and Uhami⁴, Carl Peters acquired for the Society for German Colonization the sovereign rights and the private ownership over extensive territories. The chiefs received presents and promises of 'protection'. The Society of course, was at that time in no position to protect anybody in East Africa. The territory acquired in this way lay in the hinterland of the East African coast between Pangani and Kingani. It was never precisely defined but probably covered an area of about 60,000 square miles.

Carl Peters was back in Berlin on 5 February, 1885. A few weeks later the Society for German Colonization was granted an Imperial Charter in respect of its possessions in East Africa (27 February, 1885). The granting of a charter to Carl Peters and his associates at this time is difficult to understand. In November 1884 Peters had been officially informed that no imperial protection would be granted to his enterprise. Yet in the following February Bismarck granted an Imperial Charter to the Society for a purely 'paper colony'. The Society exercised no effective authority in East Africa. Neither the Society nor the Reich could protect anybody there. This was a different matter from 'protecting' Lüderitz's 'establishments' at Angra Pequeña (S.W. Africa) which could be defended from the sea.

Whatever may have been Bismarck's motives there can be no doubt that the Imperial Charter was drawn up in haste. It was a

13

very brief document. It declared that the German Emperor placed under his sovereignty and Imperial protection certain territories in East Africa. These lands were the 'lordships' of Usagara, Nguru, Useguha and Uhami which lay to the west of the coastal possessions of the Sultan of Zanzibar and were not under the authority of any other Power. The extent of these territories was not defined. The Society for German Colonization was to exercise in these territories all the rights acquired by treaties with the chiefs—that is to say all sovereign rights and the private ownership of land. It was also to be responsible (under Government supervision) for dispensing justice to natives and Europeans. The sole condition imposed upon the Society was that it should remain a German organization and that its directors should all be of German nationality.[5]

This was an unusual form of charter. It differed from contemporary British charters to colonial companies which Bismarck professed to admire. Compared with the British practice there were some striking omissions from the German charter. No provision was made concerning the internal organization of the private society which had been given very wide powers over a huge tract of territory. No obligations to refrain from establishing a trade monopoly and no duties regarding the building of roads and bridges were imposed, nor were there any provisions regarding the welfare of the natives— such as to forbid slavery or to prohibit the sale of intoxicating liquors. These omissions were astonishing since the Imperial Charter was granted on the day after the Berlin West Africa (Congo) Conference completed its labours—a conference which (under Bismarck's chairmanship) had paid careful attention to the freedom of trade, the policy of the 'open door', and the treatment of natives in central Africa.[6]

The German Government supported the Society for German Colonization both against Britain and the Sultan of Zanzibar. The Sultan declared that the territories claimed by Carl Peters fell within his dominions. In August 1885 a naval demonstration forced the Sultan to give way. By a treaty signed on 20 December, 1885, Germany secured various privileges in the harbours of Dar-es-Salaam and Pangani as well as the right to send certain goods duty free through the Sultan's coastal dominions to the German territories in the interior. Germans were in future to enjoy extra-territorial rights in the Sultan's dominions. A year later, in the autumn of 1886, the British and German governments made an agreement fixing the spheres of influence of the British and German East Africa companies. The Sultan of Zanzibar was recognized as having authority over 1,000 miles of coastline from Tungi Bay to Kipini.[7]

In the interior Germany secured a free hand to the south of a line drawn from the mouth of the 'River Umba or Wanga'[8] to Lake Jipe, and from there round the northern slopes of Mount Kilimanjaro to the Victoria Nyanza. The British sphere of influence lay to the north of Germany's territories and extended as far as a line drawn from the intersection of 10° north and 37° east to the River Tana.

Meanwhile fortune did not smile upon those who were trying to turn Germany's paper claims in East Africa into realities. First, there were sharp differences to be overcome between those who were interested in the exploitation of the lands acquired by Carl Peters and the two Hamburg commercial houses (Hansing & Co. and William O'Swald) which had long been established at Zanzibar. These differences were settled at a conference in Berlin in September 1885. The Hamburg firms agreed to take over the commercial activities of Carl Peters in Zanzibar on a commission basis. In the interior the East Africa Company was free to establish its own trading stations. Secondly, it was necessary to devise an administrative organization to direct operations in Germany. A committee appointed by a Society which anybody could join by paying a few marks was hardly suitable for this purpose. Thirdly, more money was urgently needed if the interior of East Africa were to be successfully exploited.

Various explanations have been put forward to account for the difficulties experienced in setting up in Germany an organization capable of supervising the administration of the newly acquired territories in East Africa. It has been suggested that the German legal system did not make adequate provision for organizations that combined commercial privileges with the exercise of wide administrative powers over colonial territories.[9] But the South West Africa Company—which had no charter—had become a corporation according to Prussian law in April 1885 and had in this way secured the rights of a 'legal person'. This proved to be a satisfactory form of organization. The East Africa Company did not follow suit until March 1887.

Two factors help to explain the reluctance of the German East Africa Company to become registered as a corporation. First, there was the unusual character of the shareholders whose financial obligations and interests varied so much. Secondly, there was the personal ambition of Carl Peters to secure a form of organization which would give him as much authority as possible.

On 12 February, 1885, a committee of the Society for German Colonization appointed 'a directorate of five members for fifteen years which should have the sole responsibility of exercising the rights secured in Africa'. The directors were Carl Peters, Count Behr-Bandelin, Dr. Lange, Herr Jühlke and Consul Roghé. They proceeded to form a 'German East Africa Company'. The structure of this organization is difficult to ascertain. After summarizing statements issued by the 'Company' to explain to the German public what it was Wagner wrote that the 'Company' could not be classified under any existing legal category. He stated that this was because the company was 'something new in our history and by its exercise of both sovereign and private rights has developed beyond the range of private law'. 'In this respect it should be compared with the Congo Company rather than with any of our private companies at home'.[10]

This 'Company' appears to have consisted solely of the five directors. The shareholders were described as 'sleeping partners' who exercised no direct authority over the directors but had contracts with the 'Company'. So anomalous an organization, unknown to German law, could not survive for long. Within five weeks the directors had turned themselves into a joint-stock company called the 'German East Africa Company: Carl Peters & Associates'. It was entered in the Berlin Commercial Register. The shareholders, however, were still described as 'sleeping partners'. Shortly afterwards there were fresh changes. The posts of financial director (Lange) and commercial director (Roghé) were abolished, thus leaving Carl Peters—as managing director—virtually in sole charge of the affairs of the Company.

In the summer of 1885 a new development occurred. Karl von der Heydt—the head of a well-known Elberfeld banking house—became a shareholder and a director of the East Africa Company. Before long the Company had lost the popular character which the presence of numerous small shareholders had given it. It fell into the hands of great capitalists. There followed a struggle between those who were interested in the commercial development of the new colony and those who were interested in its political expansion. The former, represented by von der Heydt, wanted the East Africa Company to become a corporation on the lines of other privileged colonial companies. Carl Peters, on the other hand, wanted to retain as much control in his own hands as possible so as to press forward with his plans for new acquisitions in East Africa.

In the autumn of 1885 the small shareholders were bought out. On 20 March, 1886, the joint-stock company (Carl Peters and Associates) was abolished and its rights were transferred to a 'provisional syndicate' whose task was to set up a corporation under Prussian law. On 27 March, 1887, the King of Prussia granted the

East Africa Company rights of incorporation. Incorporation under Imperial Law was possible after March 1888 and the Company secured such incorporation in 1889. Thus after many vicissitudes the organization of the East Africa Company received a permanent form. The attempt of Carl Peters to dominate the affairs of the Company had failed and the big financiers were in control.

This did not mean, however, that the financial problems of the Company had been solved. Between October 1884 and 31 December, 1886, the Company had spent 700,000 marks. Another 700,000 marks were needed for capital expenditure and 400,000 marks for running expenses. The newly incorporated East Africa Company took over liabilities amounting to 1,320,000 marks.[11] Although bankers like von der Heydt were now interested in the Company it was still difficult to raise new capital. It is said that little progress was made until Bismarck induced the Overseas Trading Corporation (the *Seehandlung*)—a State financial institution linked with the Reichsbank—to set an example by subscribing 500,000 marks. Then 2,000,000 marks was subscribed by a group of Berlin bankers.[12] Even this could hardly be described as enough capital for the exploitation of a large colony and does not compare favourably with the £240,000 initial capital subscribed by the founders of the British East Africa Company.

The years 1885-7 were thus a period of considerable uncertainty in the affairs of those interested in the East African enterprise. At home their organization was unstable and did not secure a permanent form until March 1887. New capital flowed in with exasperating slowness. In East Africa the first Anglo-German agreement upon spheres of influence was not concluded until October 1886 and that was no final settlement. In the circumstances the East Africa Company might well have pursued a cautious policy and contented itself with taking preliminary steps, with the somewhat scanty means at its disposal, to develop the regions covered by Carl Peters's treaties and the Imperial Charter.

Such a policy did not suit Carl Peters. A mere 60,000 square miles gave no sufficient scope to his immense ambitions. He dreamed of a vast German empire in Africa which should stretch far beyond his original acquisitions. He embarked upon what is called his *Politik der Überstürzung*—that is to say a determined effort to forestall foreign rivals by an aggressive policy of rapid land-grabbing in East Africa. Sixteen expeditions[13] were undertaken for this purpose in 1885-6. Some visited territories which subsequently fell within the frontiers of German East Africa, but others went further afield to Somaliland, Nyasaland, British East Africa and Comoro Island.

By the end of 1886 Carl Peters was claiming territories as large as British India stretching from the Upper Nile to the Limpopo. Eventually, of course, nothing came of these grandiose plans but the expeditions of 1885-6 dissipated the energies and resources of the East Africa Company at a critical stage in its career.

The establishment of effective authority in the hinterland by the German East Africa Company depended upon finding a solution to the problems created by the fact that the Sultan of Zanzibar held the whole of the coastline. By holding the ports the Arabs could tax and control all trade between the outside world and the German colony. The Company was in a dilemma. It had no army or police force of its own. Consequently if the Company failed to secure the co-operation of the Sultan it would be forced to appeal to the authorities at home for help. After Said Bargash's death his successor Said Kalifa came to an agreement with the Germans in 1888.[14] He leased the collection of customs duties on the coast to the German East Africa Company for fifty years in return for an immediate payment of 50,000 rupees. Subsequent annual payments were not to exceed 170,000 rupees. The Company also received a five per cent. commission on the net revenue derived from customs duties. In addition the Company secured certain privileges in the coastal region such as the exclusive right to mine minerals, to regulate commerce, to build roads, railways and canals, and to erect telegraphs. The nominal sovereignty of the Sultan over the coastal strip remained and the administrative functions exercised by the Company were carried out in his name. For practical purposes, however, the keys to the interior—seven harbours and three roadsteads—were now in German hands.

At the same time Carl Peters was trying to obtain for the German East Africa Company some real measure of control over the hinterland by means of the establishment of 'stations'. Although the Imperial Charter had given sovereign powers to the Society for German Colonization only in respect of those territories covered by treaties secured by Carl Peters's first expedition it was tacitly assumed by the Company—and no one seems to have challenged the assumption—that it might exercise similar rights over the whole of the German sphere of influence in East Africa. Carl Peters arranged for the founding of 'stations' both inside and beyond the territories (never precisely defined) which he had secured in 1884. By 1887 ten 'stations' had been established—three in the Kingani valley, one on the River Wami (in the Useguha district), two in Usagara, two in the Pangani valley, one on the coast near the British frontier and one at Bagamojo.

18

Count Pfeil visited these posts in 1887 and observed that there was little possibility of rapid economic progress being made by the establishment of plantations. His judgement was sound. This early attempt to grow tobacco and other tropical and sub-tropical products and to use the stations as centres for collecting such native products as ivory and rubber was a costly failure. In 1888—at the time of the Arab revolt—the German East Africa Company reduced its 'economic' stations to two and concentrated its attention upon trading on the coast rather than upon running plantations. But still economic progress was disappointingly slow. In 1892 Germany's exports to her East African colony amounted to only just over 2,000,000 marks and imports from East Africa were valued at only 200,000 marks.[15]

These developments—the establishing of the Company's authority on the coast and the setting up of trading posts and plantations in the interior—led to an Arab rising which threatened to drive the Germans out of East Africa altogether. Recent encroachments upon the commercial activities—particularly the slave-trading—of the Arabs and the undermining of the authority of the Sultan of Zanzibar had made serious inroads upon the power of the Arabs in East Africa.

Led by Bushiri the Arabs rose in revolt against the Germans. The Company was in a difficult position. It had no army and no police force. Tiny detachments of *askari* had occasionally been raised on the coast to deal with minor disturbances in the hinterland. If more serious trouble arose the officials of the Company on the coast had to rely upon landing parties sent from German warships for protection. The first attacks upon German customs officials took place in August 1888 and by the end of that year the East Africa Company was unable to collect customs duties or to carry out any administrative functions on the coast.[16]

The East Africa Company appealed to Bismarck for military assistance. Within four years of the inauguration of his colonial policy Bismarck was faced with the very situation that he had sought to avoid. A colonial company was incapable of exercising the administrative functions with which it had been entrusted and was asking for military assistance to establish its position. Bismarck had frequently defended his colonial policy by declaring that chartered companies would defray the necessary administrative and military expenses overseas: that those who profited from colonies would pay for their upkeep. Now he had to ask the German taxpayer to provide funds for a military expedition to assert the authority of the East Africa Company. Refusal to intervene would have involved the Reich in a serious loss of prestige.

Fortunately for Bismarck there was a factor in the situation which enabled him to secure both funds from the Reichstag and the naval assistance from Britain. He was able to gain support both at home and abroad from the very people who least approved of Germany's entry into the colonial field. The Arabs were slave dealers. It was by stressing the fact that the defeat of the Arabs would mean the end of the slave trade in East Africa that Bismarck secured help from such unexpected quarters. He went so far as to argue that the suppression of the slave trade and not the rescue of the East Africa Company was the object of the proposed expedition to East Africa. In November 1888 Germany secured the co-operation of Britain in establishing a joint naval blockade of the East African coast. In January 1889 the Reichstag voted 2,000,000 marks to put down the slave trade and to protect German interests in East Africa. Captain Wissmann was appointed Imperial Commissioner in German East Africa and was given command of the expeditionary force to suppress the slave trade and establish law and order.

Wissmann arrived in Zanzibar at the end of March 1889. Shortly afterwards by agreement with the East Africa Company he was given control over both the military operations and the civil administration. Only the administration of the customs remained in the Company's hands. For practical purposes this marked the end of the Company's career as a body exercising sovereign rights. Early in 1891 Wissmann, in a final report on his expedition, announced that the Arab rising had been completely suppressed. The cost to the German Government had been considerable. The 2,000,000 marks voted in January 1889 had proved to be insufficient. Another 2,000,000 marks was voted by the Reichstag in the autumn of 1889 and a further 4,500,000 marks in May 1890. But the authorities in East Africa spent more than this and no statement of accounts showing how the money had been spent was submitted.

By this time the frontiers of German East Africa had been settled by Anglo-German treaties signed in June and July 1890. Germany accepted a northern frontier which excluded her from the Upper Nile region. Britain obtained a free hand in Uganda. Germany surrendered her shadowy 'protectorate' over Witu and so gave up her attempt to establish a new colony north of the British sphere of influence. Germany secured a common frontier with the Congo Free State and so frustrated Cecil Rhodes's plan of a Cape to Cairo route entirely under British control. Germany accepted the establishment of a British protectorate over Zanzibar and Pemba. Britain ceded the island of Heligoland to Germany.

This settlement of colonial frontiers and the suppression of the

Arabs made it possible for the German Government to come to a new arrangement with the German East Africa Company (29 November, 1890). The Government took over full responsibility for the government of the colony and the administrative functions of the Company came to an end. The rights acquired by the Company from the Sultan of Zanzibar in 1888 were made over to the German Government. In return the Government gave the Company both money and privileges. The Company received 60,000 marks a year (out of East African customs revenue) to be used as interest and repayment of capital on a loan of 1,000,000 marks. About two-fifths of the proceeds of the loan was required to compensate the Sultan of Zanzibar. The remaining three-fifths was virtually a gift from the Government to the Company. Further, important economic privileges were granted to the Company such as the monopoly of mining minerals, of owning unoccupied land, and of establishing a bank of issue.[17]

The reasons for the failure of the German East Africa Company to administer the colony successfully may be summarized as follows. The Imperial Charter was given in the first place to an organization which had no resources or experience and was wholly incapable of exercising sovereign rights over a vast stretch of African territory. Owing largely to rivalry between Carl Peters and the bankers who alone could provide the funds necessary to open up a new territory some time elapsed before the East Africa Company was organized as a joint stock company. Lack of money made it impossible to establish law and order in the interior of East Africa. Precious funds were wasted on expeditions to extend the frontiers of the colony. The plantations of the Company were also a failure and it was realized that in the initial stages of colonization commerce rather than plantations should be fostered. But the opposition of the great German trading houses at Zanzibar made it difficult for the Company to develop its commerce. Above all the Company could not hope to establish its position in the interior until the power of the Arabs on the coast had been broken. Only the State had the resources to do this and so the Company's sovereignty collapsed almost before it was born.

New Guinea Company,[18] 1884-1899

The acquisition of German colonies in New Guinea, the Bismarck Archipelago and the Marshall Islands owed much to the untiring energy of Adolf von Hansemann, the head of the *Disconto-Gesellschaft* (Discount Company) which was one of the big German banks.

He was largely responsible for the successful floating of the *Deutsche Handels- and Plantagen-Gesellschaft in der Südsee* (1880) which took over the trading establishments in the Pacific of the Hamburg firm of Johann Cesar Godeffroy which was in financial difficulties.

In April 1883 Hansemann tried to persuade the firm of Robertson & Hernsheim, which also traded in the Pacific, to co-operate in the establishment of a new company to open up New Guinea. When these efforts failed Hansemann and his associates purchased from Baring (London) those shares of the *Handels- und Plantagen-Gesell-schaft* which were in English hands. On 26 May, 1884, Hansemann took the lead in establishing the New Guinea Company (with a capital of 6,000,000 marks) and sent Dr. Otto Finsch to New Guinea to prepare the way for the establishment of a German colony there. On 27 June, 1884, Hansemann and Bleichröder asked Bismarck for Imperial protection for any possessions that Finsch might acquire.

On 20 August, 1884, those interested in the New Guinea enterprise were officially informed that they might expect the same Imperial protection for lands secured in New Guinea as had been given to German merchants who had signed treaties with native chiefs in West Africa. On the previous day, von Oertzen, the German Imperial Commissioner in New Britain, had been told to annex such territories on the north-west of New Guinea as were not in Dutch or British hands. Oertzen gave every assistance to Finsch who explored 1,000 miles of the north coast of New Guinea in the autumn of 1884. Finsch signed treaties with native chiefs at Port Constantine and elsewhere.[19] Then German gunboats appeared on the scene and the German flag was raised at Finschhafen and Friedrich Wilhelmshafen. In April 1885 Britain and Germany agreed on the extent of their spheres of influence in New Guinea. Germany secured nearly a quarter of New Guinea in the north-east of the island (Kaiser Wilhelmsland)[20] and several groups of islands collectively known as the Bismarck Archipelago.[21]

By this time the New Guinea Company had secured the co-operation of the firm of Robertson & Hernsheim and had been granted sovereign rights over most of the newly acquired German possessions in the western Pacific. The Imperial Charter granted to the New Guinea Company on 17 May, 1885, was an improvement in two respects upon that granted a few weeks earlier to Carl Peters and his associates in East Africa. First, the area in which the Company was to exercise its privileges was precisely defined. Its rights were confined to German New Guinea and to the Bismarck Archipelago—that is to say the German sphere of influence already agreed upon by Herbert Bismarck and Lord Granville and shortly to be embodied in a formal exchange of notes. Secondly, the charter contained a reference to the intention of the German government to foster the welfare of the natives. A second charter was granted to the New Guinea Company on 13 December, 1886, with respect to those of the Solomon Islands which fell within the German sphere of influence under the Anglo-German agreement signed in the previous April.

By its first charter the New Guinea Company was allowed to exercise sovereign rights in Kaiser Wilhelmsland and the Bismarck Archipelago. It was authorized to sign treaties with native chiefs and to take possession of all unoccupied land. These privileges were to be exercised under the supervision of the Imperial Government which would make regulations to safeguard both existing property rights of third parties and the welfare of the native population. A condition imposed upon the Company was that all its directors should be German citizens.

So great were the difficulties experienced by the New Guinea Company in establishing an orderly administration[22] and developing the colony from an economic point of view that after only four years it surrendered its sovereign powers to the Government. On 1 November, 1889, the Government agreed to accept full responsibility for the government of German New Guinea and the Company promised to defray the costs of the administration. This arrangement—which was much the same as the agreement of 1888 between the German Government and the Jaluit Company for the administration of the Marshall Islands—lasted until 1892. Then the New Guinea Company resumed its sovereign powers. Again the Company was unable either to govern the colony satisfactorily or to run its plantations at a profit.

In 1895 the German Government was once more prepared to relieve the Company of its administrative duties but in the following year the Reichstag refused to ratify the agreement since the proposed financial arrangements were alleged to be too favourable to the Company. It was not until October 1898 that a new agreement was made between the Government and the New Guinea Company. By this agreement, which came into force in October, 1899, the Company gave up both its sovereign rights and various monopolies. In return the New Guinea Company received the sum of 4,000,000 marks payable in ten equal annual instalments and a grant of 150,000 hectares of land.[23] Altogether the New Guinea Company had exercised sovereign powers for nine years.

The reasons for the failure of the New Guinea Company to govern the colony successfully are not far to seek. The location of German

New Guinea was unfavourable to its development as a colony. The Dutch half of the island shared in the economic expansion of other parts of Holland's empire in the East Indies. The British colony (Papua) had commercial contacts with Queensland. But Kaiser Wilhelmsland was isolated. It had few links with world trade routes and its economic progress was necessarily slow. An attempt to establish a regular connexion between German New Guinea and Cooktown failed as several vessels were lost and in 1888 the New Guinea Company sent its ships to Soerabaya (in the Dutch East Indies) where contact with Europe was maintained by the Dutch Stoomvaart Maatschappij Nederland.[24]

A great range of mountains ran along the centre of New Guinea and in the German colony the hills came close to the mangrove swamps and coral terraces of the coast. In the valleys of the rivers—such as the Sepik and the Ramu—were unhealthy swampy flatlands. Mountains, swamps and jungles retarded efforts to open up the interior. New Guinea lay in the tropics and its hot, moist climate was enervating to Europeans. Disease, rains and floods hampered economic exploitation. The treacherous coast and great gales impeded shipping. Few of the aboriginal natives survived. Europeans came into contact with Melanesian immigrants on the coast and Papuans in the interior. The differences between the two peoples were linguistic rather than racial. Both were in a low stage of development. Many of the natives were addicted to cannibalism. Their small tribes were divided by forests and mountains and there were no large social groupings of natives. Blood thirsty feuds were not uncommon. The natives heartily disliked their European conquerors but were too divided among themselves to offer united resistance to the Germans.

The Bismarck Archipelago was, in many ways, similar to New Guinea. Here, too, mountains and forests made penetration into the interior very difficult. The Melanesian inhabitants were hostile and by no means easy to handle. The sparsely populated Gazelle Peninsula of New Britain (Neu Pommern)—the seat of early European trading factories—was the only part of the archipelago well known to the Germans. Here—first at Herbertshöhe (1890-9) and then at Rabaul—was the seat of the Company's administration for the whole of the archipelago.

The early efforts of the New Guinea Company to develop the economic resources of New Guinea and the Bismarck Archipelago were unsuccessful. Its attempts to establish tobacco, cotton and coffee plantations broke down. Lack of skill and experience on the part of overseers and officials, failure to secure competent native

24

labourers, native hostility, adverse weather conditions and floods, and the loss of steamers helped to account for the Company's failures. In the early 1890's the trading stations at Finschhafen, Hatzfeldhafen and Butaneng and the plantation at Marago had to be given up. Malaria had carried off nearly all the Europeans living in Finschhafen (1891).[25] In 1898, at the close of its career as a company wielding administrative and judicial authority, the New Guinea Company had only three main trading stations and four subsidiary commercial agencies in New Guinea. Seventy-one Europeans were employed. In the Bismarck Archipelago, on the other hand, the Company was more active since it maintained five main trading stations and a network of seventy-two subsidiary commercial agencies employing ninety-one Europeans. In 1899 the cost of administering German New Guinea and the Bismarck Archipelago was 640,000 marks but the revenue raised by the colony amounted to only 80,000 marks.

The directors of the New Guinea Company had many excuses to offer for the slow progress that was made in setting up an efficient system of administration, in establishing profitable plantations, and in encouraging trade. They blamed their English and Australian trade rivals, they blamed the natives who proved to be singularly unco-operative, they blamed the malaria which killed off their employees and the high seas which sank their ships, they blamed investors at home who would not find the money for the establishment of new colonial enterprises. But Adolf von Hansemann and his colleagues were slow to realize to what extent the remedies lay in their own hands. The board of directors of the New Guinea Company had adopted too centralized an organization. Decisions which should have been taken on the spot were referred to headquarters in Berlin. The Company employed inexperienced officials who did not possess the qualities necessary for the efficient conduct of affairs. Above all the activities of the Company, in the 1890's, were on far too small a scale and the capital at its disposal was quite inadequate.

THE JALUIT COMPANY, 1888-1906

By the 1870's German merchants—the most important being J. C. Godeffroy and Robertson & Hernsheim—had established several trading stations in the Marshall Islands in the western Pacific. In 1878 a German gunboat (the *Ariadne*) visited the Ellice Islands and the Duke of York Islands and the Marshall Islands. Treaties were signed with native rulers which gave Germany the right to establish a coaling station at Jaluit. In October 1885 the gunboat *Nautilus* appeared at Jaluit to raise the German flag and to take formal possession of the Marshall, Brown and Providence Islands. Bismarck tried to persuade the firm of Robertson & Hernsheim to accept full responsibility for the administration of these territories. Robertson, however, made it clear to the Chancellor that the firm was unwilling to accept a charter since the financial responsibilities would be too heavy.

For three years the Imperial Commissioner in the Marshall Islands was without a budget or a staff. Eventually at the end of 1887 progress towards a solution of the problem was made by the establishment of a new joint-stock company to operate plantations and to trade in the Marshall Islands, Gilbert Islands and Caroline Islands. This was the Jaluit Company[26] which was founded by the two firms which had already established the New Guinea Company. These firms were the German Trading and Commercial Company in the South Seas[27] and Robertson & Hernsheim. The former was supported by the bankers Adolf von Hansemann and von Bleichröder. From its headquarters at Apia in Samoa the German trading and Commercial Company in the South Seas continued its large-scale trading activities in those parts of the Pacific lying outside the spheres of interest of the New Guinea and Jaluit companies. The firm of Robertson & Hernsheim had grown out of the pioneer exploring and commercial activities of the brothers Eduard and Franz Hernsheim.

Like Robertson & Hernsheim a few years previously, the Jaluit Company declined to accept an Imperial Charter empowering the Company to exercise sovereign rights over the Marshall Islands. The Company did, however, agree to take some measure of responsibility for the future administration of the islands. An agreement was signed on 21 January, 1888, by which the Jaluit Company promised to defray the expenses of the administration of the Marshall Islands, the Brown Islands and the Providence Islands[28] by Imperial colonial officials. The Jaluit Company estimated that the initial cost of establishing an administration would be 90,000 marks[29] and that expenses in the future would amount to 83,000 marks a year.[30] These estimates show that in 1888 the Jáluit Company imagined that it could administer the Marshall Islands with a staff of eight—a governor, a secretary and six policemen. In return the German Government allowed the Company to appropriate unoccupied land and to monopolize both the exploitation of the Namorik pearl-fisheries and the export of guano from Bikar. The Government promised that the Imperial Commissioner would, as far as possible, follow the advice of the Jaluit Company with regard to any edicts which he might issue, particularly those concerning the imposition of taxes or duties. It was also agreed that Imperial laws and regulations affecting the Marshall Islands should not be promulgated until the board of directors of the Jaluit Company had been given an opportunity of examining them and expressing an opinion upon them.

The arrangements made in 1888 worked very satisfactorily for eighteen years. In the Marshall Islands the representatives of the Jaluit Company and the colonial officials worked well together. Although the cost of administration increased they did not prove to be an unduly heavy burden on the resources of the Company.[31] The annual budget was drawn up by the senior colonial official in consultation with the Jaluit Company. Since the Company had to meet any deficit in the budget it also enjoyed the right of receiving a surplus. The income of the colonial administration was derived from a native tax in kind (360,000 lb. of copra per annum); a uniform head tax of twenty marks payable by each adult white resident, a graduated turnover tax on local trading companies,[32] and a shipping tax payable by vessels not owned by local firms.

The native Polynesian inhabitants were peaceful folk who caused their new masters no difficulty. They gave up their arms in 1898 and law and order reigned in the Marshall Islands. The development of this German colony was not retarded by any native risings.

When Germany purchased the Caroline Islands from Spain in 1899, after the Spanish-American war, the Jaluit Company apparently found no difficulty in contributing towards the additional expenses involved in administering these new possessions. With the aid of a government subsidy the Jaluit Company now maintained a regular mail service by the steamship *Germania* between the German possessions in the western Pacific (the Marshall Islands, the Marianne Islands, the Caroline Islands and the Bismarck Archipelago) and Hong Kong and Sydney.

The Jaluit Company was very successful as a commercial concern. A French writer declared in 1905 that it was 'la plus prospère de toutes les sociétés coloniales allemandes'.[33] It began its career in 1888 with ten trading stations. Three years later the value of German trade with the Marshall Islands was double that of the trade of the United States and eight times as large as that of Britain. The acquisition of two rival American and British concerns—A. Crawford & Co. and the Pacific Island Co.—virtually gave the Jaluit Company a monopoly of the commerce of the Marshall Islands. In the late 1880's it appeared that the main economic resources of these islands would be guano and pearls. In fact the

27

Jaluit Company gained little advantage from its monopoly of the exploitation of these two products.

It was the expansion of the copra trade which eventually laid the foundations of the success of the Jaluit Company and brought high dividends to the shareholders. Coconut plantations were established in the islands of Eniwetok,[34] Mile, Likiëb[35] and Ujelang. In 1903 it was reported that the plantations in the Marshall Islands covered an area of 2,480 hectares—coconuts being raised on 1,125 hectares—employing 177 native workers. Exports of copra from the islands in the early twentieth century varied from 3,000 to 3,500 tons a year. In 1905 the value of the copra exported was nearly 700,000 marks. About half of the copra was sent to Germany and the remainder was imported by Australia and Chile. In 1901 the Jaluit Company (capital: 1,200,000 marks) made a net profit of 179,798 marks and paid a dividend of 12 per cent. In 1903 the dividend rose to 15 per cent. and in 1906 to 20 per cent.[36] At this time the Jaluit Company maintained 4 main trading stations and 93 subsidiary agencies. Most of the trading posts were in the Marshall Islands and Caroline Islands but 24 were situated in the Gilbert Islands, which were a British possession. The Jaluit Company employed between 70 and 80 persons.[37]

The privileged position of the Jaluit Company was brought to an end on the initiative of the German Government in 1906. This action was taken because the colonial officials in the Marshall Islands became involved in a dispute with the Australian Government which threatened to endanger satisfactory relations between Germany and Britain. In 1904 the Sydney shipping firm of Burns, Philip & Co. extended one of its services to the Gilbert, Ellice and Marshall Islands. The officials in the Marshall Islands, acting in accordance with the agreement made in 1888 between the German Government and the Jaluit Company, made the Australian firm pay licences on its ships using German harbours and also levied a duty of thirty marks upon every ton of copra exported. The Australian Government complained that these taxes infringed the Anglo-German Treaty of 10 April, 1886, which had provided for equal treatment of British and German traders in the colonial possessions of both Powers in the Pacific. There was obviously much force in the Australian case.

The German Government replied that its agreement with the Jaluit Company had been in force since 1888 and that for seventeen years no foreign Power had complained of the commercial privileges enjoyed by the company. It was also alleged that the Australian Government was itself infringing the spirit—if not the letter—of the

Anglo-German Treaty of 1886 by subsidizing the firm of Burns, Philip & Co. The German Government reduced the taxes of which the Australian Government complained. The Australians, however, were not satisfied.

In the circumstances the German Government decided to terminate its agreement with the Jaluit Company. On 1 April, 1906, the Government assumed full financial responsibility for the administration of the Marshall Islands. The Jaluit Company became a purely commercial concern. It retained, however, certain privileges regarding the exploitation of guano and phosphate deposits. The German Government removed the discriminating duties which had been the subject of complaints.[38] In future the Marshall Islands were administered as a dependency of German New Guinea.

In conclusion the reasons for the failure of Bismarck's attempt to govern the German colonies by means of chartered companies may be briefly summarized. In theory, no doubt, there were strong arguments in favour of the idea that commercial establishments which had been trading for many years on the African coasts and in the Pacific had the experience necessary to undertake administrative functions in newly acquired territories. In practice the merchants of Hamburg and Bremen were unwilling to accept such responsibilities. New colonial companies established with the support of the big banks—such as the German S.W. Africa Colonial Company—were equally reluctant to shoulder administrative responsibilities. Bismarck had to bring considerable pressure to bear on the New Guinea Company to induce it to accept a charter. The Jaluit Company would not undertake administrative responsibilities although it did agree to pay the cost of governing the Marshall Islands. In East Africa Bismarck granted sovereign powers to a private association—the German Colonial Society—which had very little money and no experience in administration. It was some time before a joint-stock company was founded to take over from the German Colonial Society the duty of administering the new colony in East Africa.

The two companies which did have administrative responsibilities in East Africa and New Guinea failed because of lack of money and lack of experience. German investors were reluctant to support colonial companies and for some time neither the East Africa Company nor the New Guinea Company possessed sufficient capital for its needs. The officials employed by the two companies were inexperienced. Some of them were mere adventurers who were quite unfitted for the tasks that they were supposed to perform. The hostility of the natives hampered the establishment of an orderly administration in New Guinea while the opposition of the Arabs on the coast prevented the East Africa Company from establishing plantations and maintaining law and order in the hinterland. Only the Jaluit Company, with its flourishing trade in copra, was able to pay for the administration of the Marshall Islands for eighteen years. This was the only successful application of Bismarck's principle that the merchants and shippers who profited from colonial trade should bear the cost of administering new overseas possessions.

REFERENCES

1. For Bismarck's colonial policy and his views on the administration of overseas territories see Kurt Herrfurth, *Fürst Bismarck und die Kolonial-politik* (1917) and Maximilian von Hagen, *Bismarcks Kolonialpolitik* (1923). See also P. Décharme, *Compagnies et sociétés coloniales allemandes* (1903).
2. The German S.W. Africa Colonial Company was founded in April 1885. Its chief financial supporters were the *Diskontogesellschaft* (Adolf von Hansemann), the *Deutsche Bank* and the banker Bleichröder. The Company firmly refused to accept the administrative powers which Bismarck wished to confer upon it. All that it did was to exercise very limited administrative functions for a short time on parts of the coast of S.W. Africa. In 1889 Herbert Bismarck declared: 'Our S.W. African Company is stagnant, bankrupt and hopeless'. For this company see L. Sander, *Geschichte der deutschen Kolonialgesellschaft für Süd-West Afrika . . .* (2 vols., 1912).
3. For the German East Africa Company see Bruno Kurtze, *Die Deutsch-Ostafrikanische Gesellschaft* (1913), and an article by R. von Spalding in the *Deutsches Kolonial Lexikon* (3 vols., 1920), Vol. I, pp. 408-410.
4. Some of these treaties are printed by J. Wagner, *Deutsch-Ostafrika . . .* (1888) and by Bruno Kurtze, op. cit., pp. 178-181.
5. For English translations of the Charter see Sir Edward Hertslet, *The Map of Africa by Treaty* (edition of 1894) p. 303 and R. Coupland, *The Exploitation of East Africa, 1856-90* (1939), p. 405.
6. Shortly afterwards (6 March, 1885) Count Münster informed Lord Granville that the territories mentioned in the Imperial Charter granted to Carl Peters and his associates fell within the extended zone of the conventional Congo Basin (Berlin Congo Act).
7. The authority of the Sultan of Zanzibar was recognized as extending twenty sea miles inland from the coast.
8. There is a River Umba but there is no 'River Wanga'. The Wanga is a creek. There is a village called Wanga two miles north of the River Umba. The frontier at this point had to be defined more precisely later.
9. See Veit Simon, 'Deutsche Kolonialgesellschaften' in the *Zeitschrift für das gesamte Handelsrecht*, Vol. XXXIV, Heft i and ii.
10. J. Wagner, *Deutsch Ost-Afrika . . .* (1888) p. 61 and p. 77.
11. Alfred Zimmermann, *Geschichte der deutschen Kolonialpolitik*, (1914), p. 129 (note 22) citing the *Hamburger Korrespondent*, 7 February, 1887.
12. Robert Warschauer, Mendelsohn-Bartholdy, Delbrück.
13. See list in Bruno Kurtze, op. cit., pp. 14-15.

14. The agreement of 1888 is printed in Bruno Kurtze, op. cit., pp. 163-170.
15. See tables at the end of Otto Mayer, *Die Entwicklung der Handelsbeziehungen Deutschlands zu seinen Kolonien* (1913).
16. For the Arab rising of 1888 and its suppression see Rochus Schmidt, *Geschichte des Araberaufstandes in Ostafrika* (1892) and an article by R. von Spalding in the *Deutsches Kolonial Lexikon* (3 vols., 1920), Vol. I, pp. 68-71.
17. The agreement between the German Government and the German East Africa Company is printed in Bruno Kurtze, op. cit., Appendix VIII, pp. 193-6.
18. For the New Guinea Company see *Nachrichten über Kaiser Wilhelms Land und den Bismarcksarchipel* (fourteen annual reports of the New Guinea Company issued in three volumes, 1875-80), and an article by E. Krauss in the *Deutsches Kolonial Lexikon* (3 vols., 1920), Vol. II, pp. 629-31.
19. Other explorers who went to New Guinea shortly afterwards were not sent out by the New Guinea Company, but were sponsored by other organizations. Zöller and Hellwig were sent out by a newspaper (the *Kölnische Zeitung*) to travel in the Finisterre Mountains. For Zöller's own account of the expedition see H. Zöller, *Deutsch Neuguinea und meine Ersteigung des Finisterregebirges* (1891). Lauterbach was sent by the Colonial Society (*Kolonial-Gesellschaft*) to explore the course of the River Gogol (or Weu). For this expedition see an article in the *Deutsche Kolonial Zeitung*, 24 February, 1898.
20. German New Guinea had an area of 179,000 square kilometres.
21. The Bismarck Archipelago and the Solomon Islands had an area of 61,000 square kilometres.
22. See Table 1 in Appendix.
23. For a criticism of this agreement by Hans Blum, a former employee of the New Guinea Company, see the *Deutsches Wochenblatt*, 4 February, 1899. The Company replied in a pamphlet entitled: *Der Vertrag zwischen dem Reich und der Neu Guinea-Kompagnie* (Berlin, 1899).
24. In 1893 the German Government paid the North German Lloyd Company of Bremen an annual subsidy of 250,000 marks to maintain a regular service between German New Guinea and Singapore.
25. W. von Hanneken, a former official in German New Guinea, gave a depressing account of the miserable condition of the colony in the early 1890's in articles published in *Die Nation* 1895, Numbers 9 and 10. Adolf von Hansemann replied to these criticisms in an article published in the same journal (*Die Nation*, 1895, Number 16).
26. For the Jaluit Company see an article by E. Krauss in the *Deutsches Kolonial Lexikon* (3 vols., 1920), vol. II, pp. 122-3.
27. For the *Deutsche Handels- und Plantagen-Gesellschaft* see an article by E. Krauss in the *Deutsches Kolonial Lexikon*, vol. I, pp. 300-1. This firm had been established on 16 March, 1878, with an initial capital of 5,000,000 marks which was later reduced to 2,750,000 marks. It had taken over the plantations and trading establishments of the well-known Hamburg firm of Johann Cesar Godeffroy when it was in financial difficulties. The house of Godeffroy had opened up German trade in the Pacific in the 1850's. Its able agents Unshelm (who died in 1864) and Theodor Weber (popularly known as the 'South Sea King') established a virtual monopoly of the export of copra from Samoa. For the firm of Godeffroy see an article in the *Deutsches Kolonial Lexikon*, vol. I, p. 742, Sylvia Masterman, *The Origins of International Rivalry in Samoa, 1845-84* (1934), and R. Hertz, *Das Hamburger Seehandelshaus J. C. Godeffroy & Sohn* (1922).

28. Nauru Island (formerly known as 'Pleasant Island') which was annexed by Germany in April 1888 also fell within the sphere of interests of the Jaluit Company. It was not until 1906 that the valuable phosphate deposits on this island were developed by an English company (the Pacific Phosphate Company). The German Government gave the Jaluit Company permission to make over to the Pacific Phosphate Company its exclusive rights to exploit the phosphate deposits on Nauru. The Jaluit Company held some shares in the Pacific Phosphate Company.

29. See Table 2 in Appendix.

30. See Table 3 in Appendix.

31. See Table 4 in Appendix.

32. E.g. a turnover of more than 500,000 marks rendered a firm liable to a payment of 9,000 marks.

33. André Chéradame, *La colonisation et les colonies allemandes*, (1905), p. 406.

34. The plantations on the Eniwetok islands were cultivated by natives on behalf of the Jaluit Company.

35. The ownership of the plantation of Likiëb was divided into four equal parts—(i) one quarter owned by the Jaluit Company, (ii) one quarter owned by A. Capelle, (iii) one quarter owned by J. de Broun's successors, and (iv) one quarter owned jointly by the Jaluit Company, A. Capelle and J. de Broun's successors.

36. Dividends of the Jaluit Company:

1900	..	12 per cent.	1904	..	15 per cent.
1901	..	12 ,, ,,	1905	..	15 ,, ,,
1902	..	12 ,, ,,	1906	..	20 ,, ,,
1903	..	15 ,, ,,			

37. Not including men serving on the Company's ships.

38. See Alfred Zimmermann, *Geschichte der deutschen Kolonialpolitik* (1914), pp. 282-3. Burns, Philip & Co. claimed 250,000 marks compensation from the German Government for alleged loss of trading profits in the years 1904 and 1905. Eventually in 1908 the Company accepted the sum of 82,000 marks in final settlement of its claims.

Chapter III

ECONOMIC ASPECTS OF GERMAN COLONIZATION

GERMANY'S demand for the return of the colonies which she held before the first World War was an important factor in Anglo-German relations in the 1930's. It was to Britain that Germany addressed herself, although many of her former possessions were held as mandates by Dominions of the British Empire—South Africa, Australia and New Zealand—and by other countries such as France, Belgium and Japan.[1]

Hitler, in his Reichstag speech of 20 February, 1938, declared that 'the claim for German colonial possessions will . . . be voiced from year to year with increasing vigour . . . Possessions which Germany did not take away from other countries and which today are almost of no value to these Powers, appear indispensable to our people . . . We do not want credits, but a foundation to live which enables us to secure national existence by our own diligence.'

It was frequently asserted in the 1930's that overseas possessions of the type held by Germany before 1914 were of value to the parent country by providing opportunities for the settlement of 'surplus' population, for the purchase of important raw materials and food-stuffs, and for the sale of manufactured articles. It is proposed to examine these arguments in the light of Germany's experience before 1914. First it will be necessary to ascertain the financial cost of the colonies to Germany, and secondly an attempt will be made to discover the extent of the economic advantages secured by the Reich from its overseas possessions.

The cost of acquiring and maintaining overseas possessions was considerable. By the end of the fiscal year 1906 Germany had spent about £32,000,000 more on her colonies than had been collected there in revenue and to this must be added £1,000,000 paid to Spain for the Caroline, Pelew and Marianne Islands (except Guam), and the large sums spent in putting down native risings. Between 1908 and 1913, colonial deficits amounted to £15,000,000. Further, over £11,000,000 had been raised in colonial loans which were generally guaranteed by the home government. These totals do not include numerous items—such as shipping subsidies and naval expenditure—at least part of which was money spent in encouraging

33

colonial trade and in defending overseas possessions. In the period 1884-1914 colonial budget deficits and subsidies had cost Germany over £50,000,000, and the total cost to the German taxpayer of the colonies between 1884 and 1914 could hardly have been less than £100,000,000.

By 1914, not one of the principal colonies balanced its budget. South West Africa, for example, received £3,396,000 in contributions from the Reich in the last five years before the occupation of the territory by South African troops; and this was at a time when the mining industry was prosperous. In the same period, £3,463,000 was spent by the German Government on the armed forces of the colony. Only Samoa and Togoland received no subsidies. It had been argued that this inability to balance colonial budgets was not surprising, and that some losses must inevitably be incurred in the early stages of opening up 'new' regions. But the financial position of the colonies continued to be unsatisfactory after Germany lost them. Between 1920 and 1934, South West Africa received £2,360,000 in loans from the Government of the Union of South Africa, and over £1,000,000 of capital expenditure had been undertaken on the South West African railways. It is stated that between the two World Wars the British Government gave, lent or guaranteed £9,500,000 to Tanganyika alone.[2]

The colonies never absorbed a large number of German settlers. In 1903 there were only 5,125 Germans (including 1,567 officials and soldiers) in the colonies. Ten years later (1 January, 1913) there were 19,696 Germans in the African and Pacific colonies; over three thousand of them were soldiers or policemen. Kiao Chow, according to a census of 1910, had a German population of 3,806, including 2,275 members of the military and naval forces. The total German population of the colonies was therefore about 23,500. Half of them (12,292) were in South West Africa; in East Africa there were 4,107 Germans; in the Cameroons 1,643; and in the Pacific islands 1,645. The number of Germans living in the former colonies in 1934 was 16,774, of whom about 12,000 were in South West Africa. The reduction in the number of German residents in the former colonies has been due partly to the expulsion of Germans by the mandatory Powers, under Article 122 of the Treaty of Versailles; from South West Africa, however, only the military and a few persons considered to be undesirable were repatriated. Moreover, new German immigrants were later admitted; consequently there were in 1938 rather more Germans in South West Africa than there had been before 1914.

An examination of the structure of the white population in the three largest African colonies before 1914 shows how small was the number of farmers and planters who might, with their families, be regarded as permanent settlers, as compared with the officials, soldiers, policemen and merchants for whom the colonies were only a temporary home.[3]

The Germans living in the colonies before 1914 were only a tiny fraction of those who emigrated from Germany. The total number of emigrants between 1887 and 1906 was 1,085,124, and most of them (1,007,574) went to the United States of America. Between 1925 and 1934 the total emigration from Germany amounted to 38,343 persons, and a mere two-and-a-half per cent. of this number went to Africa. The German emigrant preferred to go to an industrial country with a high standard of living rather than to tropical or semi-tropical colonies. It may be observed that, of the 22,000 volunteers who served in the campaign against the Herero at the beginning of this century, only five per cent. accepted the offer of the German Government of financial assistance to establish themselves permanently in South West Africa as farmers. Geographical and economic conditions made it impossible for the former German colonies to support large white populations. They were commercial and plantation regions rather than colonies of settlement.[4]

The main reasons why Germany's possessions overseas proved to be unattractive to emigrants were the unhealthiness of the tropical colonies, the infertility of large regions of those colonies in which settlement was possible, the considerable amount of capital required to establish a plantation or farm, the difficulties of transport and the uncertainty concerning the land and native policies of the German Government. The position with regard to health and fertility was summed up by the German colonial governor, who declared that 'the fertile colonies are unhealthy, the healthy colonies are infertile.' In South West Africa, for example, the Namib and Kalahari deserts are useless for settlement. Over forty thousand square miles of this cu.. ..y are virtually uninhabitable. The account of the campaign against the Herero, which is reproduced by Gustav Frenssen in *Peter Moors Fahrt nach Südwest: Ein Feldzugsbericht*, gave a terrible picture of the hardships of travelling and fighting in South West Africa. The unhealthiness of tropical colonies naturally deterred settlement. Malaria, blackwater fever and dysentery were the curse of the West African colonies. The official report on Togoland for 1910-11, for example, stated that the condition of the health of Europeans in Lome, the capital, had been extremely unfavourable (*äusserst ungünstig*) in that year, on account of exceptionally heavy rains. But strenuous efforts were made to improve the health of white people, natives and stock. Dr. Robert Koch made important researches on the problem of sleeping sickness in East Africa.

The high cost of settling in the colonies was made clear in a reply of the emigration department of the German Colonial Society to the inquiry of a prospective settler. 'The German colonies are not suited to the reception of settlers with no means or even with little. A large amount of capital and knowledge of tropical agriculture are both requisite. In South West Africa, which is chiefly suited for cattle breeding, at least £1,000 or £1,350 has hitherto been regarded as necessary. The laying down of cocoa plantations in Samoa requires a capital of at least £2,500. Only in the German East African territories of West Usambara and Langenburg, and in the Marianne Islands, is settlement possible with about £500, to which must be added the costs of transport and equipment. A warning must be given against emigration to any of the German colonies for the purpose of settlement without the requisite financial resources.'⁵

Lack of adequate transport facilities checks settlement. Progress in this respect was somewhat slow in the German colonies. Private capital was seldom available and the Reichstag was reluctant to make the necessary grants. In 1906, for example, it rejected the proposal that it should subsidize a railway line in South West Africa. At the end of 1906 only 1,175 miles of railways had been built. Lack of communication made it difficult to deal with native risings. The economic value of railway construction in Africa was clearly demonstrated when the English built the line from Mombasa to Nairobi and Kisumu on Victoria Nyanza. This benefited not only British East Africa (Kenya) and Uganda, but also the northern portion of German East Africa. The total value of the trade of the German ports on the Victoria Nyanza rose from £22,669 in 1903— when the Uganda Railway was completed—to £494,381 in 1910. Considerable progress in the building of railways in the German colonies was made after 1906. Dr. Dernburg, who was in charge of German colonial affairs between 1906 and 1910,⁶ succeeded in more than doubling the railway mileage during his period of office. The 780-mile Central Railway from Dar-es-Salaam to Kigoma on Lake Tanganyika was finished in 1914. By 1914 about 2,800 miles of railways had been built in the German colonies, and the Shantung lines amounted to 300 miles.

The native policy of the German Government affected the terms upon which planters and farmers could secure land and labour. In the early days of the colonies little attention was, on the whole, paid to the welfare of the natives. Huge land concessions were made to companies at the natives' expense. The exaction of forced labour was not uncommon. These and other grievances led to risings. In South West Africa the rebellion of the Herero and other tribes was mercilessly suppressed. There, declared Professor Bonn, 'we solved the native problem by smashing tribal life and by creating a scarcity of labour.' During the 'new era' of German colonization inaugurated by Dr. Dernburg, a different native policy was pursued in some colonies, and an attempt was made to preserve native ownership of land and to foster native production of tropical raw materials and foodstuffs. This led to serious controversies between the colonists and Government officials in certain colonies. Albrecht von Rechenberg, Governor of East Africa from 1906 to 1912, was bitterly criticized on account of the new policy which was leading to an increase in the area of land under native cultivation. In the Cameroons, on the other hand, little attempt was made to turn over a new leaf with regard to native policy. The Duala tribe was so incensed at the loss of lands at the mouth of the River Wurri in 1913 that, a year later, it joined the British when they invaded the colony at the outbreak of the war. So long as uncertainty prevailed concerning the future of the Government's land and native policies, the colonies were hardly likely to prove attractive to settlers.

Since the colonies were unsuitable for large-scale white immigration, it was natural that Germans should hope to recover the money sunk in them by trade. Germany did not endeavour to monopolize colonial trade. East Africa lay within the Congo basin, as defined by international agreement in 1885, and here the principle of the 'open door' was pursued in conformity with the Congo Act. In other colonies, too, Germany did not, on the whole, pursue an exclusive policy. She did, however, encourage shipping to the colonies by subsidies.[7] Colonial tariffs were drawn up mainly to raise revenue, though an element of protection was not entirely absent. Tsingtau was a free port, and in 1906 a form of customs union was established between the German (leased) territory of Kiao Chow and the Chinese province of Shantung. Efforts were made to foster colonial production by an intensive study of the problems of tropical agriculture. The Amani Institute in East Africa, for example, has been described as 'a tropical scientific institute superior to anything in the British colonies or protectorates, and comparable with Pusa in India or the Dutch establishment at Buitenzorg in Java.'[8]

The trade of the colonies did not make as much progress as had been expected. Some of the factors that hindered commercial development were the lack of capital in the early days of colonization, the serious native risings—such as the Majimaji rebellion in

East Africa, 1904-7—and the reluctance of the Reichstag to vote money for railway building. In the twenty years between 1894 and 1913, the value of Germany's trade with her overseas possessions, including Kiao Chow, totalled £48,000,000, or an average annual sum of £2,400,000. At the time of the 'colonial scandals' of 1906, Bebel observed that 'if Germany should lose all her trade with Denmark (£15,000,000 in 1905), it would mean much more than if all her colonial trade (£3,200,000) went to the devil.'⁹ Colonial commerce was increasing in the decade before the war : whereas in 1904 Germany's colonial trade amounted to only three- and three-quarter million pounds, by 1913 it had risen to thirteen million pounds. But even this was only a half per cent. of the country's total commerce.

Trade between an industrial country and newly opened-up tropical possessions overseas normally takes the form of an exchange of manufactured articles for foodstuffs and raw materials. In 1913 the German colonies (excluding Kiao Chow) imported merchandise—including gold and silver—to the value of £7,853,000, and 37.8 per cent. of this came from the Fatherland. Only four-fifths of one per cent. of Germany's total exports went to her colonies. Before 1914 War, Germany supplied East Africa with a little over half (51.3 per cent. in 1912), and South West Africa with well over three-quarters (81 per cent. in 1913), of the goods they imported. After the loss of the colonies, Germany's share in the imports of these territories declined. In 1935, for example, Tanganyika obtained only one-tenth (10.7 per cent.) of her imports from Germany.

Colonial enthusiasts asserted that Germany's overseas possessions would supply her with considerable quantities of tropical foodstuffs and raw materials which could not be produced at home. These sanguine hopes were not fulfilled. In 1913 the German colonies (excluding Kiao Chow) exported merchandise—including gold and silver—to the value of £8,100,000. Only a third of these exports went to the Fatherland, and they amounted to only a half per cent. of Germany's total imports.

The chief products of the former German colonies may be briefly summarized. The Cameroons and Togoland produced rubber, ivory, cotton, palm-oil and kernels, copra, timber, bananas and cocoa. One of East Africa's principal exports was sisal hemp, of which 16,000 tons were produced in 1912. Considerable progress in the production of sisal hemp was made after 1918. Production rose from 46,462 tons in 1929, to 84,000 tons in 1935. It was a non-native crop and the quality and length of the fibre were excellent. Cotton, coffee, copra, ground nuts, ivory, hides and skins were also exported from this colony. South West Africa's economic wealth lay in its mineral resources (diamonds, copper, lead and vanadium), in agricultural products (cattle, wool and hides), and in guano. The value of the diamonds produced in 1911 was £1,250,000. In 1927 diamonds to the value of £1,620,000 were produced. A decline in production followed between 1928 and 1933. Germany's possessions in the Pacific produced phosphates, cocoa, copra, palm-oil and kernels. The valuable phosphate deposits of Nauru were exploited after 1906 by an English company: 138,725 tons were exported in 1913. Twenty-one years later, 418,950 tons of phosphates were produced in Nauru. It may be observed that Germany's former colonies lacked completely or produced only small quantities of the six raw materials which Dr. Goebbels has considered to be essential for an industrial State—namely, coal, iron, oil, cotton, rubber and copper. Both before and after the first World War, Germany secured only a very small proportion of her tropical foodstuffs and raw materials from the colonies.[10]

Germany's efforts to increase the amount of cotton produced in her overseas possessions may serve as an example of the difficulty of securing adequate quantities of raw materials from her colonies. Germany had a large and important cotton industry, and the value of her imports of raw cotton rose from £11,500,000 in 1897 to £25,000,000 in 1907. Most of this cotton came from the United States of America, India and Egypt. In the hope of reducing the country's dependence upon foreign sources of supply, the German Colonial Economic Committee sent out a mission to Togoland in 1900. There were no crown lands in this colony, so attempts were made to encourage natives to grow cotton. A cotton experimental station (and agricultural training school for natives) was established by the Committee at Nuatjä in 1904, and this was taken over by the Government in 1908. The cotton exports of this colony were over half a million pounds (weight) in 1911. On the eve of the first World War, however, a German export admitted that there was little hope of any substantial increase in Togoland's production of cotton. In East Africa the Colonial Economic Committee began to encourage cotton culture in 1902. Here it was cotton grown by white planters that was fostered by small subsidies by the Committee on thé Rufiji River in 1907. By 1912, nearly forty thousand acres were under cotton, and about four million pounds (weight) were exported. In other colonies, cotton production was of little importance. In the Cameroons the natives of the Lake Chad region grew cotton for their own use but not for export; Kiao Chow exported a small amount from Shantung province.[11]

The comparatively slow economic progress of the colonies helps to explain the reluctance of German financiers to invest money in them. Considerable Government encouragement—such as guaranteeing interest, granting various privileges and providing subsidies—was necessary to induce bankers and others to advance money for colonial undertakings.[12] Even so, the capital forthcoming was inadequate, and English financiers played an important part in opening up some of the colonies, particularly South West Africa.[13]

It has been shown that Germany spent at least a hundred million pounds in obtaining and running her colonial empire. To a small section of the population the colonies were doubtless a source of profit; the merchants and planters who exploited the natural and human resources of overseas possessions; the shipping companies which secured subsidies; the civil and military officials who obtained posts—all had every reason to support colonial enterprise. But the German people as a whole gained little economic advantage in return for the money spent. The overseas possessions contained a mere 23,500 Germans before 1914; German settlers went to the Americas rather than to the colonies; German capital was attracted more quickly to the gold-mines of South Africa than to the diamond fields of South West Africa; the trade of the parent country with the colonies amounted to only a half per cent. of Germany's total trade; and not one of the principal colonies was financially self-supporting.

It was argued that it was unfair to rely upon these statistics of colonial settlement, trade and finance, since in 1914 Germany had held her overseas possessions for only thirty years, and had not had time to develop them adequately. On the other hand, by 1938 the regions in question had been in European hands for half a century and there still seemed little prospect of large-scale white settlement or of startling commercial progress. Germans argued that this was due to neglect on the part of the mandatory Powers. There was perhaps some substance in this argument. The Report of the East African Commission of 1925, for example, admitted that in Tanganyika 'in such matters as education, medical work and scientific research, the pre-war standard has not yet been reached'. The same report stated that in 1925 the Amani Institute was 'for all practical purposes lying derelict'. But other factors must also be taken into consideration. Lack of progress had been due partly to difficulties of reconstruction after 1918—particularly in Tanganyika—and partly to geographical, economic and social conditions in the territories. Factors such as unhealthy climate (as in the West African colonies), lack of water (as in many parts of South West Africa), difficulties of

communication, and the existence of native land and labour problems stood in the way of the fulfilment of the hopes of the colonial
enthusiasts who thought that 'if Germany were in possession of
colonies of her own, her balance of trade and her currency would
be immensely improved.'[14] As the writer of a pamphlet on *Raw
Materials and Colonies* observed, 'the dissatisfied Powers tend, con-
sciously or unconsciously, to over-estimate the economic advantages
of colonial changes; . . . the cure for their difficulties is world-wide
rather than colonial in scope.'[15] The proportion of the raw materials
and of foodstuffs exported from the former overseas possessions
which Germany consumed in 1938—compared with her total consumption—could be raised by increasing production from these
regions or by decreasing imports from the colonial territories of
other Powers. Both developments would have been possible. The
first would have been expensive and the results might well have
proved disappointing; the second would have been in keeping with
Hitler's policy of *Autarkie*—the attempt to secure national self-
sufficiency at all costs.

It was frequently asserted in the 1930's that Germany would
benefit by the recovery of overseas possessions, because she would
then be able to pay for colonial raw materials and foodstuffs with
her own currency instead of having to do so in foreign money which
she then had such difficulty in acquiring.[16] In the first place, it may
be observed that the shortage of foreign currency was partly due to
the fact that in Hitler's day Germany preferred to devote a considerable part of her resources to the purchase of materials needed by her
vast armament industry rather than to the acquisition of colonial
products. Secondly, the ability to pay for raw materials in a German
colony with German money depended upon the willingness of the
exporter to accept that currency. The money would be of use to
him only if it enabled him to purchase goods that he required. If he
were forced to accept German currency he might be entirely dependent upon Germany for the goods he needed. The currency argument
virtually assumed that the trade of German colonies would be a
complete German monopoly. This would raise the cost of living in
the colonies and that, in turn, would increase the price of colonial
raw materials and foodstuffs—which was just what Germany desired
to avoid. Moreover, in the Congo basin (as defined by the treaty of
1885), and in regions held under League of Nations' mandate, there
were legal difficulties in the way of establishing a complete monopoly
of colonial trade.

There was another economic problem that deserves mention.
Whatever justice there may have been in German claims for the

return of her colonies in the 1930's, she had obviously no right to obtain, without making compensation, the capital invested by foreign Governments and private persons in these territories since 1918. More than £25,000,000 had been invested in Tanganyika alone. If Germany had purchased all foreign investments, the cost would have been very great; if she had not done so, she would have failed to secure that monopoly of colonial trade that she obviously desired.

From a purely economic point of view, one might have expected the mandatory Powers to be anxious to get rid of the territories as quickly as possible; and Germany might have been expected to refuse them at any price. But other factors—such as considerations of defence, and, above all, of prestige—were of great importance. If the German demand for the return of her colonies in the 1930's is to be regarded in its true light, it must be recognized that arguments based solely upon economic considerations were exaggerated, and that other motives were of greater significance.

REFERENCES

1. See Table 5 in Appendix.
2. For German colonial finance see M. E. Townsend, *The Rise and Fall of Germany's Colonial Empire* (1930), pp. 237-40 and 264-6; Bernhard Dernburg, *Koloniale Finanzprobleme* (1907); E. Volkmann, 'Finanzen,' *Deutsches Kolonial-Lexikon*, vol. i, pp. 616-625; *Report of South-West Africa Commission* (Pretoria, 1936), chap. 6; and 'Germanicus,' *Germany in the last Four Years* (1937), chap. 9.
3. For German colonial population see G. Thilenius and G. Zoepfl, 'Bevölkerung der Schutzgebiete,' *Deutsches Kolonial-Lexikon*, vol. i, pp. 195-7. The figures for 1911 are taken from the official report on the colonies (*Die Deutschen Schutzgebiete in Afrika und der Südsee, 1910-11*). For German settlement in South West Africa, see Erich Obst, 'Das Deutschtum in Süd-Afrika' and 'Das Deutschtum in Südwest-Afrika,' *Geographische Zeitschrift*, xl, 1934, pp. 190-216; for East Africa, see Paul Samassa, *Die Besiedlung Deutsch-Ostafrikas* (1909). It may be added that in the early years of the present century, when colonial enthusiasts argued that colonies were needed to absorb German settlers, Germany was a country which attracted a considerable number of immigrants. According to the census of 1905, there were over a million foreigners in Germany. In the following year, there were in Prussia alone 240,000 foreign workers on the land, and 360,000 engaged in industrial pursuits. See Moritz Bonn, *Nationale Kolonialpolitik* (1910), pp. 4-5. See Table 4 in Appendix.
4. Some German writers on the colonial question recognized this and did not exaggerate the value of the former overseas possessions as areas of settlement. Johannsen and Kraft, for example, wrote that 'the use of colonies for European settlement . . . plays a subordinate part only, in so far as Germany is concerned. The suggestion that large numbers of Germans should take up their permanent residence in the German-owned overseas territories, either as farmers or in other capacities, is rejected for social as well as racial reasons . . .' (*Germany's Colonial Problem* (1937), p. 49).

5. Quoted by W. H. Dawson, *The Evolution of Modern Germany* (1911), p. 395.
6. Dr. Dernburg was placed temporarily in charge of colonial affairs in September 1906. Between May 1907 and June 1910 he was at the head of the newly established Imperial Colonial Office.
7. The following companies received subsidies: North German Lloyd (for lines to eastern Asia, Australia and New Guinea), German East Africa Line (for lines to East and South Africa), Jaluit Company (for ships on the Sydney-Jaluit-Hamburg route), Woermann Line (for ships between Cape Town and South West Africa), and Hamburg-America Line (for ships on the Shanghai-Kiao Chow route).
8. *Report of the East Africa Commission*, April 1925, p. 86.
9. Quoted by M. E. Townsend, op. cit., p. 238.
10. For colonial economic development, see the annual reports of the Imperial Colonial Office; articles in the *Deutsches Kolonial-Lexikon* on separate colonies, tropical products and companies engaged in colonial activities; and the following: Hermann Paasche, *Deutsch-Ostafrika: wirtschaftliche Studien* (1906); Paul Samassa, *Die Besiedlung Deutsch-Ostafrikas* (1909); P. Rohrbach, *Deutsche Kolonialwirtschaft*, vol. i, *Südwestafrikas* (1907); T. Hoppe, *Wirtschaftsstruktur und Wirtschaftsentwicklung Deutsch-Südwestafrika* (1936); a report of the Chamber of Commerce for the Southern Cameroons entitled *Der Handel in Südkamerun in den Jahren 1908 bis 1911*; A. F. Calvert, *German East Africa* (1917); William Churchill, 'Germany's Lost Pacific Empire,' *Geogr. Rev.*, x (1920), pp. 84-90. The economic position of the former German colonies in 1936 was discussed by Ludwig Schoen, *Das koloniale Deutschland*, a collection of articles which appeared in the Berlin *Börsen-Zeitung*, 1937.
11. For German colonial cotton production, see *Die Baumwollfrage, Veröffentlichungen des Reichskolonialamts*, No. I (1911); *Der Baumwollbau in den deutschen Schutzgebieten; seine Entwicklung seit dem Jahre 1910, Veröffentlichungen des Reichskolonialamts*, No. 6 (1914); M. Schanz, *Cotton Growing in German Colonies* (Manchester, 1910).
12. See Herbert Feis, *Europe, the World's Banker*, 1870-1914, pp. 181-3 (1930).
13. M. E. Townsend, op. cit., pp. 170-71; and articles in the *Kolonial-Lexikon*, vol. i, pp. 376-81.
14. Johannsen and Kraft, op. cit., p. 38.
15. Information Department Papers, No. 18, Royal Institute of International Affairs (1936).
16. Lionel Birch observed that 'not all countries with colonies (or mandated territories) have the same currency as their colonies (or mandated territories). Great Britain is a case in point. The sterling currency does *not* prevail in Palestine or Kenya, and various other Crown colonies or mandates. Even where, as in some Dominions, it does prevail (*e.g.* in Australia and New Zealand), there have been of recent years, and still are, heavy "agios" with London—sometimes as much as 50 per cent. This is equivalent to a depreciation of the local currency' (*The Demand for Colonies*, 1936, p. 21).

Chapter IV

GERMANY'S TRADE WITH HER COLONIES, 1884-1914

WHEN Hitler established the Third Reich his demand for the return of the German colonies[1] gave a new interest to the study of the economic structure of those territories before the first World War. One aspect of this problem—the commercial relations between Germany and her overseas possessions—overshadowed all others because the establishment and development of the German colonial empire was, above all, a commercial venture.

It is true that when the colonies were acquired it was thought that some of them would become regions of white settlement that might attract German immigrants. The drive for German colonies coincided with a rapid increase in population and an exceptional wave of emigration. The population rose from 41 millions in 1871 to nearly 50 millions in 1890 and the proportion of the total population living in urban communities of more than 2,000 persons increased in the same period from 31.6 per cent. to 42.5 per cent. The birthrate per 1,000 of the population (excluding stillbirths) reached the high level of 39.2 in the period between 1876 and 1880. The increase in population came at a time of industrial depression and more Germans than ever before left the country. In the three years 1880-2, half a million people emigrated and most of them settled in the United States. It was natural that colonial enthusiasts should hope that the possessions overseas which Germany secured between 1884 and 1890 would attract a part of this stream of emigrants. But they were disappointed, for the colonies proved to be unsuitable for large-scale white settlement. The unhealthy tropical climate of the Cameroons and Togoland, the lack of water in parts of South West Africa, the long absence of adequate communications, the reluctance of capitalists to invest in colonial enterprises, and the hostility of many of the native tribes were some of the factors which discouraged settlement. Over a million Germans emigrated between 1887 and 1906, and, as in the early eighties, they nearly all went to the U.S.A. By the early years of the present century, however, the emigration problem had ceased to be a serious one. In 1900 only 22,000 Germans emigrated. Indeed emigration was now counterbalanced by

44

the immigration of foreigners. In 1905 there were over a million foreigners in Germany. Some were agricultural labourers in the eastern provinces of Prussia, while others were industrial workers in the Rhineland manufacturing region. There were only about 23,500 Germans in the colonies in 1913, half of them being in South West Africa. Many were not permanent settlers but were civil servants, soldiers and policemen.[1]

The more obvious it became that the colonies were of little use from the point of view of settlement the greater was the stress laid upon their commercial value. They were regarded as potential reservoirs of raw materials for German industries and as future markets for the products of German factories. An inquiry into the extent to which these hopes had been realized by 1914 is hindered by two difficulties.

First, the subject is one upon which there have been many controversies in Germany from the days when Ludwig Bamberger denounced Bismarck's colonial policy in the eighties to the time of the violent discussions on Bernhard Dernburg's colonial reforms in 1907-10. These controversies have left a legacy of tendentious literature which does not lighten the task of the student.

Secondly, there are numerous difficulties in using German colonial commercial statistics. Not until 1902 were imports and exports recorded in the same way for all the colonies (except Kiao Chow) and for the earlier period the statistics are defective. Thus the trade statistics of some colonies were grouped together and not given separately. Even after 1902 the statistics should be used with caution. It is, for example, difficult to discover the extent of the export of German goods to German colonies. The statistics give the value of goods sent from Germany to the colonies, but they do not state the country of origin. Some exports—such as petrol and rice—were obviously not produced in Germany though they were shipped from a German port. Consequently it must be recognized that only tentative conclusions concerning Germany's colonial trade may be drawn from an examination of the commercial statistics.[2]

A study of the economic development of the colonies shows that it was not the settler but the merchant who was the pioneer in these regions. In West and East Africa and in the Pacific it was the great trading houses of Hamburg and Bremen that paved the way for colonization. In South West Africa in the sixties and seventies the German missionaries were engaged not only in cultural work but in commercial activities. In Germany itself it was merchants such as J. C. Godeffroy and Adolf Woermann and bankers such as von

45

Hansemann and Bleichröder who played a not unimportant part in winning Bismarck over to a colonial policy.

Although the German colonial empire was not founded until 1884, Germans had long been active in overseas commerce. In the later middle ages the Hanse merchants had dominated the trade of the Baltic and North Sea for a time. In the sixteenth century German merchants and bankers had a share in Spanish and Portuguese colonial enterprise and the Welsers governed part of Venezuela in 1528-46.[4] In the last quarter of the seventeenth century the Great Elector of Brandenburg established trading factories on the West African coast.[5] In the eighteenth century the Austrian East India Company (1721) had trading stations in the East Indies for a brief period and Joseph II held the Nicobar Islands in 1778-85. But these commercial colonial ventures failed because of the jealousy of other powers and the lack of a strong central government capable of protecting and stimulating overseas trade. In some respects conditions were little better after 1815. The country was divided into nearly forty states and neither the Germanic Confederation (1815) nor the Zollverein (1834) fostered colonial enterprise. But there were no serious wars in Germany between 1815 and 1866, and those that accompanied the establishment of national unity had few adverse effects upon overseas commerce. This gave the merchants of Hamburg and Bremen an opportunity to lay the commercial foundations of the future colonial empire.[6]

Hamburg's trade with Africa developed in the forties and fifties. On the East African coast Zanzibar was the principal centre of international commerce.[7] Indian merchants had established close trading connexions with the Arabs on the island and the neighbouring mainland. The chief exports of East Africa were slaves and ivory. In 1844 Adolf Jacob Hertz, of Hamburg, sent a ship to Zanzibar and recognized the possibility of trading in cowries which could be purchased cheaply on the island. These shells found a ready market on the West African coast where they were used as currency.[8] Wm. O'Swald & Co. soon entered this branch of trade in co-operation with Captain Lorenz Diederichsen. In 1849 the firm established its first warehouse in Zanzibar and, despite numerous difficulties, its trade prospered. In 1853 O'Swald & Co. bought Diederichsen's factory at Lagos, and in 1857 an establishment was set up in Madagascar, but the centre of the firm's activities continued to be in Zanzibar.[9] Here German trade was fostered by the conclusion in 1855 of a commercial agreement between the Hanse Towns and the Sultan. Other merchant houses, such as Hansing &

Co., sent agents to the island. In the sixties and seventies the German firms competed successfully with their English rivals. The Indian merchants, however, maintained their influential position. It was estimated that in 1869-71 German firms secured 22.2 per cent. of Zanzibar's foreign commerce. American firms secured 23.2 per cent.; French 16.7 per cent.; British 15.4 per cent.; and Indian and Arab firms 21.4 per cent.

On the West African coast the principal commercial activity in the first half of the nineteenth century consisted in the export of slaves, a trade in which the Portuguese played a leading part. After the suppression of the slave trade, English and other European merchants supplied natives with salt, gin and various manufactured articles in return for such tropical products as palm-oil and kernels. European merchants had difficulty in getting into direct touch with natives in the interior since the tribes on the coast had a monopoly of the transit trade. It has been seen that Hertz, Diederichsen and O'Swald were engaged in the cowrie trade on the West African coast in the forties. The German firm which eventually exercised the greatest influence there, however, was the Hamburg house of Woermann. In 1849-50 Carl Woermann and C. Goedelt agreed to trade together on this coast, Goedelt acting as Woermann's shipper (*cargadeur*).[10] Commerce was successfully opened up in Liberia and by the sixties Woermann had established a firm hold of the trade between Gaboon and the Cameroons. Later his packet ships maintained a regular service with Hamburg. Jantzen & Thormählen and Wölber and Broehm were other successful German firms on the West African coast, and the Basel Mission had a trading factory at Accra on the Gold Coast. In 1880 German firms (such as the Bremen house of Vietor Sons) established themselves in Togoland in the hope of evading British import duties levied on the Gold Coast. Despite the rapid progress of German commerce in West Africa the English trade with that region was still four times as great as the German in 1881.

In South West Africa Germany's early commercial contacts were of minor importance. It was generally English whalers and sealers that visited the coast from time to time and it was mainly English ships that called at the neighbouring islands for guano. In the grass and scrub lands beyond the Namib desert the trade in cattle—which were sent to Cape Town—was largely in English and Boer hands, and it was an English company that tried to exploit the copper resources of Otjimbingwe. German missionaries in Hereroland (Damaraland) and Great Namaqualand did engage in commerce, but the limited liability company which was floated in Barmen with a capital of £35,000 in 1868 to trade 'in the mission fields of the Barmen Rhine Mission' became insolvent and went into liquidation.[11]

In the South Seas,[12] as in West Africa, it was a Hamburg commercial house that prepared the way for colonization. J. C. Godeffroy & Sohn established itself in the Samoan Islands in the fifties. Its headquarters were at Apia. Under the able guidance of its agent Theodor Weber (the 'South Sea King'), the firm prospered, and secured a virtual monopoly of the export of copra (dried coconut kernels) from Samoa. Godeffroy's interests extended to several other islands in the Pacific. The brothers Hernsheim were also active in the South Seas in the seventies. The German ships trading with the Samoan and Tongan (Friendly) Islands increased from twenty-four in 1868 to fifty in 1875. The importance of commerce in the Pacific was recognized by the German Government, and this was the first branch of overseas trade to receive really vigorous encouragement from the State. Between 1876 and 1879 several treaties were signed with native rulers in the South Seas by which Germany was assured trading rights and permission to build certain coaling stations. Heinrich von Kusserow, Bismarck's chief adviser in the seventies on matters concerning overseas commerce, was to a great extent responsible for these treaties. The failure of the firm of Godeffroy in 1879 (owing to unsuccessful speculations in Europe) was a blow to German prestige in the Pacific. The Reichstag, however, refused to accept Bismarck's proposal to subsidize a company which should take over Godeffroy's debts and save the shares and property of the firm from falling into the hands of English creditors. A new German company, supported by the bankers Hansemann and Bleichröder, succeeded in keeping Godeffroy's possessions in the Pacific in German hands.

Thus in the South Seas and West Africa, and to a lesser degree in South West and East Africa, Germany had substantial commercial interests. Here was a sound foundation upon which colonial enterprise could be built. There were, of course, other factors that should not be ignored. Explorers, missionaries and scientists had done valuable pioneer work in regions which eventually became German colonies. Had it not been for the activities of adventurers like Carl Peters and Adolf Lüderitz large regions in Africa might never have come under German control. And to secure foreign recognition of Germany's colonial claims was not the work of pioneers on the spot but was the achievement of Bismarck at the conference table in Europe. But Bismarck himself was the first to stress the commercial significance of the territories overseas which he acquired in 1884-90. He desired to avoid the expense of governing colonies and wished merely to afford protection to chartered commercial companies which should themselves administer territories overseas.[18]

When the colonial empire was founded, however, Bismarck's efforts to run it as a commercial venture failed. The methods that the English had adopted in the seventeenth and eighteenth centuries were hardly suited to the conditions of the last quarter of the nineteenth century. The merchants of Hamburg and Bremen, who had long engaged in commerce in Africa and the Pacific, might have succeeded in administering successfully small coastal regions adjoining trading factories, but they had not the will, the resources or the experience to open up and govern the vast hinterlands which were secured between 1884 and 1890.[14] In the Cameroons and Togoland the trading companies never exercised administrative functions. In East Africa and New Guinea the chartered companies had surrendered their administrative functions by 1890.[15] The South West Africa Company refused to accept a charter and soon gave up certain administrative powers that it had exercised. Only the Jaluit Company exercised administrative powers in the Marshall Islands into the twentieth century: it gave them up in 1906.

The responsibility of conquering and administering the colonial empire, therefore, fell almost entirely upon the State. Bismarck's failure to secure the establishment of chartered companies, which would relieve the taxpayer of the expense of running the colonies, had unfortunate results. The chartered companies survived as commercial companies which enjoyed special rights. These privileges were normally of two kinds. First, there were exclusive rights to build railways, exploit mines and so forth. Secondly, there were cash payments from the government to the companies in return for he surrender of administrative functions, some of which had hardly been effectively exercised at all. Moreover, numerous companies which had never had administrative powers also secured substantial concessions. The policy of granting wide concessions to colonial companies was carried out to the fullest extent by Dr. Paul Kayser, who was in charge of the Colonial Section of the German Foreign Office between July 1890 and March 1894. In South West Africa in particular, enormous concessions of land, mineral rights and railway privileges were made. By 1903 nine companies controlled nearly a third of the area of this colony. The South West Africa Company Ltd.—supported mainly by English capital—secured

13,000 sq. kms. of land in the north of the colony as well as the right to build a railway from the coast to the eastern frontier by way of the Otavi copper mines.[16]

The concession policy was defended on the grounds that in no other way would capital be attracted to the colonies. But the abuses which resulted from giving private companies exclusive rights over vast territories coupled with the inefficiency of the inexperienced bureaucrats sent out from Germany to govern the colonies led to numerous native risings. The most serious were the Majimaji revolt in East Africa in 1905-6 and the Herero and Hottentot rebellions in 1904-7. Criticism of the concession companies in Germany itself came to a head when the South West African companies asked for £550,000 as compensation for losses sustained during the Herero revolt. A government commission of inquiry was set up and it reported in favour of the State purchase of lands and privileges acquired by the companies. This policy was pursued by Dr. Bernhard Dernburg, who was head of the newly established Imperial Colonial Office in 1907-10. By 1914 some success had been achieved in carrying out the commission's recommendations.

The trade of the German colonies, over which these companies had no small influence, grew between 1890 and 1914, but the results of a quarter of a century of economic exploitation were by no means startling. Neither as reservoirs of raw materials nor as markets for manufactured articles did the colonies play any significant part in Germany's economic life. In 1913 Germany's colonial trade amounted to £3,750,000, which was merely half of one per cent. of her total trade. It is proposed to examine the economic relations between Germany and her possessions overseas from the point of view, first, of the exports and, secondly, of the imports of the colonies.

The colony which had the greatest variety of products was East Africa. In the early nineties its chief products were ivory, rubber, copra and groundnuts. Then the ravages of locusts, a drought, the appearance of cattle plague (*rinderpest*) in 1894 brought about a famine which checked the economic development of the colony. The export of the natives' products fluctuated considerably and eventually declined. Work on European plantations was still in the experimental stage. Some success was achieved with cotton,[17] coffee, and, above all, sisal-hemp. In 1912 16,000 tons of sisal were produced. But attempts to introduce tobacco culture failed. In the early years of the present century the economic condition of the colony improved. Trading connexions between the colony and the

50

mother country gradually became closer. In the early days of the German occupation most of East Africa's exports went, as before, to Zanzibar, where Indian and English commercial houses had a predominant influence. Later the construction of the Uganda railway attracted some of the trade of the northern regions of German East Africa into channels under English control. But when the Germans improved the communications of their colony and increased the shipping service to Dar-es-Salaam they secured a larger share of East Africa's exports. In 1895 that share had amounted to only 10 per cent.: in 1909 it was 66 per cent.[18]

Germany's West African colonies—the Cameroons and Togoland —were her most valuable possessions from the point of view of securing raw materials for her industries. The principal exports were tropical products such as ivory, rubber, copra, palm-oil and kernels. By far the most important export from the Cameroons was rubber, which was collected by natives. Little success attended the efforts of the administration to check the wasteful native exploitation of the rubber resources of the colony. In 1910 the value of the rubber sent by the West African colonies to Germany amounted to £1,000,000. Some progress was made in developing European plantations for the production of cocoa in the Cameroons[19] and cotton in Togoland. Valuable experimental studies in problems of tropical agriculture were undertaken at the Victoria botanic gardens. Despite the pioneer activities of the house of Woermann, Germany had to face severe competition in the West African trades in the early nineties, particularly from English merchants.[20] But eventually as communications were improved Germany secured a stronger hold upon the commerce of the Cameroons and Togoland, and between 1905 and 1910 there was a considerable increase in the exports of these colonies to the mother country.[21]

South West Africa, on the other hand, was the *Schmerzenskind* of the German colonial empire. As a region of white settlement it did show some promise but from the commercial point of view the Germans had one disappointment after another. The isolation of the fertile areas between two deserts, the lack of water, the difficulties of communication and the serious native risings greatly hampered the economic development of the colony. Capitalists, merchants and shippers of London and Cape Town played an important part in the early stages of the opening up of South West Africa. The best port of the colony (Walfish Bay) was in English hands; the bulk of the exports of cattle, hides and skins went to Cape Colony and not to Germany; the copper resources of Otavi were exploited by an

English company. The value of the principal exports to Germany between 1891 and 1896 amounted to only £1,100 a year. Then the disastrous cattle plague of 1896-7 reduced the export of hides. In 1897 guano—from the Cape Cross deposits—was sent to Germany for the first time and, until 1903, this was South West Africa's chief export to the mother country. Only 10.7 per cent. of the colony's total exports went to Germany in 1903, the rest going mainly to England (12.2 per cent.) and Cape Colony (70.7 per cent.). The native risings which broke out in the north of the colony in 1904 and in the south in 1905 disorganized the economic life of South West Africa. After 1906 there was a welcome increase in Germany's trade with South West Africa. This was due to the gradual restoration of law and order, the improvement of communications, the increased production of the Otavi copper mines, and the development of the diamond industry. Diamonds were discovered in South West Africa in 1908 and two years later they accounted for three-quarters of the exports of the colony to Germany.[22]

The most significant characteristic of the economic structure of Germany's possessions in the Pacific was the great dependence upon copra as the chief article of export up to 1908. Then the great phosphate deposits of Nauru began to be worked by an English company (the Pacific Phosphate Co.) and the export of this fertilizer became of considerable importance. Much of the copra came from the plantations of the New Guinea Company in the Marshall Islands and Bismarck Archipelago and, when direct communication with Germany was secured in 1904-5 through ships of the North German Lloyd, the mother country secured a fair share of the copra trade. The phosphates, on the other hand, were for the most part sent to Australia (over 70 per cent. in 1908). Germany secured 11.6 per cent. of the phosphates in 1908 and 22.1 per cent. in 1909.

The leased Chinese territory of Kiao Chow had few resources but it was of some economic importance since many of the products of the neighbouring province of Shantung were sent to the Kiao Chow port of Tsingtau to be exported. Here again the improvement of communications played an important part in strengthening the commercial relations between the colony and the mother country. The building of Tsingtau harbour, the completion of the railway to the Shantung coal mines (1904) and the improvement of ocean shipping services drew Tsingtau an increasing share of transit traffic. In 1899 most of Shantung's raw silk was exported by way of the Chinese port of Chefoo, but in 1906 nearly half of Shantung's trade went through Tsingtau. Up to 1906 Kiao Chow's chief exports were straw-twist, raw silk and hides. The production of these articles declined after that year, owing to a fall in prices, and new exports—such as cotton and groundnuts—began to appear. The value of the total exports of Kiao Chow rose from £264,450 in 1901 to £4,014,750 in 1911.[23]

Regarding the colonial empire as a whole, it is clear that by 1914 it supplied Germany with only insignificant quantities of tropical raw materials and foodstuffs. The rubber and cocoa of the West African colonies, the sisal-hemp of East Africa, the copra and phosphates of the Pacific islands, were useful, and the discovery of the diamond wealth of South West Africa was some compensation for the failure of that colony to add materially to Germany's resources. But the production of other commodities was quite unimportant. Moreover, the total exports of the German colonies were never large enough to pay for imports. In 1901 imports exceeded exports by nearly £1,350,000; in 1912 by £3,170,000. This was disappointing, even if it be remembered that Germany held her colonies for a comparatively short time and made no attempt to monopolize their trade.[24] This was a poor return for the £100,000,000 that the German taxpayer is estimated to have paid between 1884 and 1914 to cover colonial deficits and subsidies.

The colonies were equally disappointing from the point of view of their capacity to absorb German manufactured articles.[25] As was to be expected in newly opened-up regions, a characteristic of the commercial statistics of the German colonies was the importation of goods sent by the Government to equip military forces and to construct buildings for the administration, roads, railways, harbours and bridges, and of goods sent by private traders for the equipment of plantations. As the white population increased so did the importation of those European foods and drinks which were not manufactured locally. Increased colonial commercial activity necessitated an increase in the amount of silver coins in circulation, and these were imported from the mother country.

In East Africa in 1895 nearly half of the imports (48 per cent.) came from India and only a little over a quarter (27.1 per cent.) from Germany. Natives had been accustomed to get cotton cloth and garments from Indian merchants and they continued to do so. Gradually, however, Germany's share of the goods brought to East Africa by sea increased. In 1909 her share was 46.5 per cent. while those of India and Zanzibar were 18.5 per cent. and 13.5 per cent. respectively. The West African colonies imported mainly guns, ammunition and gin in the early nineties. Subsequently the imports of these articles declined. Cotton imports came chiefly from England. The imports of South West Africa differed somewhat from those of other colonies. The white population was the largest in Germany's overseas possessions. The scattered native peoples could not afford to buy European goods, particularly after the cattle plague of 1896-7 and the ruthless suppression of the risings of 1904-7. Unusually large imports of military supplies and construction goods on government account were necessary owing to the long periods of disturbance in the colony.

Germany's exports to her possessions in the Pacific were small. High freights made it difficult for German merchants to compete with rivals from Australia and the U.S.A., whose transport costs were lower. The natives were primitive folk and their wants were few. Kiao Chow imports from Germany, too, were inconsiderable. Japan supplied North China with many manufactured goods. Cotton yarn came from Japan and India. Until 1904 Germany's exports to her Chinese territory were mainly construction goods for use in building the Shantung railway. When this line and other public works were completed and when it was no longer necessary to send large quantities of military supplies to Kiao Chow the imports of the territory declined in the years 1906-10.

Although the German colonies did not absorb large quantities of manufactured articles their imports increased steadily in the early years of the present century. The imports rose from £2,580,000 in 1901 to £13,200,000 in 1912.

There were several causes for the comparative failure of the German colonial empire as a commercial venture. The overseas possessions were, for the most part, poor territories with few natural resources. It was hardly to be expected that much business could be done with the inhabitants of the fever-ridden jungles of West Africa, the deserts of South West Africa, or the lonely islands of the Pacific. A certain success was secured in fostering production of copra, rubber, cocoa, sisal-hemp and phosphates. But only a very little cotton and tobacco were obtained from the overseas possessions and some colonial commodities were almost entirely lacking. The fact that the English held Zanzibar, Walfish Bay and the best West African harbours gave them an important trading advantage over the Germans. Moreover Germany's experience of overseas commercial activity in Africa and the South Seas before the eighties of the last century, though invaluable from the point of view of tapping regions by enterprise on the coast, was no preparation for the more difficult task of opening up the trade of the vast hinterlands. German capitalists and bankers, too, lacked the experience of English rivals in colonial affairs, and it was the English who exploited the Otavi copper mines and the Nauru phosphate deposits. The tradition of giving wide privileges to chartered companies led to the development of the concession system which had unfortunate results. A vacillating and unsatisfactory native policy led to serious risings and to labour problems. The reluctance of the Reichstag to vote money for public works, such as railways, retarded the economic development of the colonies. Some of these mistakes were remedied after the exposure of various 'colonial scandals' in 1906, and the 'new era' of German colonial administration under Bernhard Dernburg's able guidance was beginning to produce hopeful results when the outbreak of war brought it to an end in 1914.[26]

REFERENCES

1. The arguments in favour of the return of Germany's colonies were stated briefly by Heinrich Schnee, *German Colonisation Past and Future* (1926); G. Kurt Johannsen and H. H. Kraft, *Germany's Colonial Problem* (1937), and Hjalmar Schacht, 'Germany's Colonial Demand' (*Foreign Affairs*, January 1937). The arguments against were given in *The British Colonial Empire and the German Claim* (Empire Economic Union, 1937) and by André Touzet, *Le Problème Colonial et la Paix du Monde. Les Revendications Coloniales Allemandes* (Paris, 1937). Impartial surveys: Lionel Birch, *The Demand for Colonies* (League of Nations Union, 1936), and a pamphlet issued by the Royal Institute of International Affairs entitled *Germany's Claim to Colonies* (1938). See also *Raw Materials and Colonies* (Royal Institute of International Affairs, 1936); Grover Clark, *A Place in the Sun* (New York, 1936); Norman Angell, *This Have and Have-Not Business* (1936) and Moritz J. Bonn, *The Crumbling of Empire* (1938).
2. G. K. Johannsen and H. H. Kraft, p. 49.
3. For German colonial commercial statistics see Rudolf Hermann, 'Kolonialstatistik,' in F. Zahn, *Die Statistik Deutschlands . . .* (1911), II, p. 955 *et. seq.*, and K. Rathgen, 'Handelsstatistik,' in the *Deutsches Kolonial-Lexikon*, II, pp. 33-5. Colonial commercial statistics were published quarterly in the *Deutsches Kolonialblatt* and annually in the *Statistisches Handbuch des Deutschen Reiches* and *Die Deutsche Schutzgebiete in Afrika und der Südsee* (herausgegeben vom Reichs-Kolonialamt). Statistics for Kiao Chow—based upon those issued by the Chinese Maritime Customs authorities—appeared in reports issued by the German Admiralty which controlled the administration of this leased Chinese territory.
4. See Konrad Haebler, *Die überseeische Unternehmungen der Welser . . .* (1903); F. Hümmerich, *Die erste deutsche Handelsfahrt nach Indien 1505-6* (1912); and M. A. H. Fitzler, 'Der Anteil der Deutschen an der Kolonialpolitik Philip II von Spanien in Asien (*Vierteljahrschrift für Sozial- und Wirtschafts-Geschichte*, XXX, 1937, pp. 19-71).
5. See Richard Schück, *Brandenburg-Preussens Kolonialpolitik . . . 1647-1721* (two volumes, 1889).
6. See M. Coppius, *Hamburgs Bedeutung auf dem Gebiet der deutschen Kolonialpolitik* (1905).

7. For the economic activities of Zanzibar and the neighbouring East African coast before 1885, see the first volume (1885) of the *Kolonial-Politische Korrespondenz* (the organ of the German East Africa Company and the Society for German Colonisation) and Bruno Kurtze, *Die Deutsch-Ostafrikanische Gessellschaft* . . . (Jena, 1913), pp. 17-39.

8. These cowries ('light blue Zanzibars' and 'dark blue Zanzibars') were not so popular with the West African natives as the 'genuine' cowries ('live' and 'dead' Maldives), which came from the Maldive and Laccadive Islands in the Indian Ocean, but the trade in them was a profitable one. See Otto Mathies, *Hamburgs Reederei 1814-1914* (1924), p. 54 *ff.*

9. For the early history of O'Swald's activities in Africa see Ernst Hieke, 'Das hamburgische Handelshaus Wm. O'Swald & Co. und der Beginn des deutschen Afrikahandels 1848-53' (*Vierteljahrschrift für Sozial- und Wirtschafts-Geschichte*, XXX, 1937, pp. 347-74). *Cf.* Karl Brackmann, *Fünfzig Jahre deutscher Afrikaschiffahrt* (1935).

10. The agreements between Woermann and Goedelt of 24 March, 1849, and 6 April, 1850, are printed by Ernst Hieke in the *Vierteljahreschrift für Sozial- und Wirtschafts-Geschichte*, XXX, 1937, pp. 261-5.

11. For South West Africa before the German conquest see Heinrich Vedder, *Das alte Südwestafrika* (Berlin, 1934).

12. See E. Wakeman, *Report of Captain E. Wakeman to W. H. Webb on the Islands of the Samoa Group, September 20th, 1871* (New York, 1872), and R. Hertz, *Das Hamburger Seehandelshaus J. C. Godeffroy & Sohn* (Hamburg, 1922).

13. M. E. Townsend, *The Rise and Fall of Germany's Colonial Empire, 1884-1918* (New York, 1930), p. 119.

14. For the German colonial companies that exercised administrative functions for a time see above, pp. 11-32.

15. The New Guinea Company recovered its administrative functions in 1893, but gave them up again shortly afterwards.

16. For the German colonial concession companies see, for example, P. Decharme, *Compagnies et sociétés coloniales allemandes* (1903); Jäckel, *Die Landgesellschaften in den deutschen Schutzgebieten* (1909); and Hermann Hesse, *Die Landfrage und die Frage der Rechtsgültigkeit der Konzessionen in Südwestafrika* (1906).

17. For the efforts of the Colonial Economic Committee to foster cotton growing in East Africa by establishing an experimental station at Nuatjä (1904) and by subsidizing plantations at Panganja (1907) see *Die Baumwollfrage. Veröffentlichungen des Reichskolonialamts*, No. 1 (1911); *Der Baumwollbau in den deutschen Schutzgebieten. Seine Entwicklung seit dem Jahre 1910. Veröffentlichungen des Reichskolonialamts*, No. 6 (1914); and M. Schanz, *Cotton Growing in German Colonies* (1910).

18. For economic problems of German East Africa see, for example, Most, 'Die wirtschaftliche Entwicklung Deutsch-Ostafrikas, 1885-1905' (*Jahresbericht der Klosterschule Rossleben*, 1906, pp. 3-28) and Hermann Paasche, *Deutsch-Ostafrika: wirtschaftliche Studien* (1906).

19. E. J. Arnett observes that 'the cocoa industry began in German Cameroons and in British Gold Coast at about the same time. The two governments put their money on very different horses in the race, and in less than ten years' time the race was decisively won by the British. While the British

backed the native farmer, the German Government backed large plantation companies, and expropriated the natives from all the best land . . .' (*Scottish Geographical Magazine*, LIV, May 1938, p. 163).

20. Ships visiting ports of Germany's West African colonies:

The Cameroons		Togoland	
		1890	
43 German ships	(40,268 tons)	58 German ships	(69,262 tons)
40 English ,,	(51,855 ,,)	52 English ,,	(47,890 ,,)
		1892	
26 German ,,	(36,285 ,,)	66 German ,,	(69,761 ,,)
38 English ,,	(51,442 ,,)	63 English ,,	(76,831 ,,)

(Otto Mayer, p. 71.)

21. Otto Mayer, p. 77. *Cf. Der Handel in Südkamerun . . . 1908-11* (Report of Chamber of Commerce for the Southern Cameroons, 1912).

22. Otto Mayer, pp. 84-92. See also Paul Rohrbach, *Deutsche Kolonialwirtschaft*, I, *Südwest-Afrika* (1907) and T. Hoppe, *Wirtschaftsstruktur und Wirtschaftsentwicklung Deutsche-Südwestafrika* (1936).

23. Ibid., pp. 108-12. See also F. Wertheimer, *Deutsche Leistungen und deutsche Aufgaben in China* (1913).

24. East Africa, the south-eastern corner of the Old Cameroons and most of the New Cameroons formed part of the Congo Basin as defined by the Congo Act of 1885, and in these regions the policy of the 'open door' was followed in conformity with treaty obligations. Elsewhere, too, tariffs were generally imposed for revenue and not protective purposes. Certain steamship lines to the colonies, however, were subsidized.

25. For the imports of German colonies see Otto Mayer, pp. 113-74.

26. See Tables 7, 8 and 9 in Appendix.

Chapter V

BRITISH ECONOMIC ACTIVITY IN THE GERMAN COLONIES, 1884-1914

A FEATURE of the development of Germany's overseas possessions between 1884 and 1914 was the way in which economic progress was hampered by lack of capital. The German investing public seldom supported colonial ventures. An analysis of the distribution of the long-term foreign investment of the Reich in 1914 shows that more German money was invested in Europe than in all other continents together. German investments in Africa (including the Reich's colonies) were only two-thirds of those in Austria-Hungary.[1] And in Africa the mines of the Rand had in the nineties attracted as much German capital as was sunk (by 1914) by private investors in all Germany's colonies.[2] The reluctance of the German public to invest in colonial enterprises may be illustrated by the experience of the first syndicate formed to build the Northern Railway in the Cameroons. It required £850,000. Preference shares, without any government guarantee of interest, proved to be difficult to place, and only £300,000 was raised in this way.[3] Even the vigorous propaganda of Dr. Dernburg, the former Director of the Darmstadt Bank who was Colonial Minister in 1907-10, had only a limited success in inducing German capitalists to support colonial enterprises.[4]

There were two main reasons why German capital was not forthcoming. First, German investors were not accustomed to put their money into colonial companies. Outside Germany they tended to favour enterprises near at hand in central and eastern Europe. German financial houses had little experience of dealing with plantation and mining companies overseas. Adolph von Hansemann, the head of the Discount Company of Berlin, stood apart from his banking colleagues in his readiness to support colonial enterprises. The merchants of Hamburg and Bremen, who might have been expected to have invested money in the colonies, on the whole confined their attention to shipping and trading ventures. The opening up of the hinterland lay outside their experience and they hesitated to embark upon new types of business. The Reichstag failed to give private investors a lead. It was reluctant to finance railway construction to foster the colonies' economic development. There was a striking contrast between the colonial railway policies of Britain and Germany. In 1903 Britain completed the Uganda Railway, which was built out of public funds. Germany, in her East African colony, had no comparable line until 1914 when the Central Railway (from Dar-es-Salaam to Kigoma) was finished.

Secondly, the German colonies did not at first appear to be promising fields for investment. Law and order were only slowly established. The blunders of German officials were largely responsible for continued trouble with the natives. Twenty years after the founding of the overseas possessions, Germany's three principal African colonies were either in revolt or in a state of unrest. In South West Africa the Bondelswarts, the Herero and the Hottentots revolted in 1903-4. In East Africa the Majimaji rising occurred in 1905. In the Cameroons the natives of the Duala district, the political and commercial centre of the colony, informed the Reichstag of their grievances in 1905 and secured the recall of Jesko von Puttkamer, the governor of the colony.

After the natives had been subdued geographical and economic factors hindered progress. Many of the territories were unhealthy and unsuitable for European settlers. South West Africa had vast tracts of desert, while in East Africa nearly two-thirds of the colony was virtually uninhabitable owing to the unsatisfactory water supply.[5]

It was some time before the staple products of the German colonies were exploited. Diamonds were not found in South West Africa until 1908. Rubber became of importance in the Cameroons only in the twentieth century. The value of the colony's rubber exports rose from £61,700 in 1891 to £573,611 in 1912. Sisal-hemp was just beginning to be of significance in East Africa towards the end of the German régime. Only 16,000 tons were produced in 1912 as compared with 84,000 in 1935.

There were consequently opportunities for foreign capital to assist in the opening up of Germany's overseas possessions. British investors helped to finance enterprises in the German colonies, particularly in the Cameroons and in South West Africa. British plantation companies alone had a capital of £1,138,000.[6]

The value of the direct trade between Britain and the German colonies in 1910 was nearly £630,000, over two-thirds of which was with West African territories (£469,000). There was also a lively commerce between Germany's overseas possessions and neighbouring British colonies. Thus the annual trade between German East Africa and Zanzibar amounted to £385,965, and that between German South West Africa and the Union of South Africa amounted to £388,300 (1910). Before diamonds were found in South West Africa one of the chief exports of the colony was cattle and they were entirely absorbed by the Cape Colony market.[7] There was also some trade between British and German possessions in the Pacific. The value of the annual trade between the German colonies and the British Empire as a whole was about £1,500,000.[8]

In 1913 there were over 300 Englishmen, mainly traders, planters and missionaries, in Germany's overseas possessions. There were also just over 2,000 persons from British colonies in those territories. Most of them were Boer farmers in South West Africa. It has been suggested that 'foreign merchants were disinclined to settle in the German colonies whose rigid rule and stiff social system were uncongenial to them'.[9]

There were two reasons why British investors showed some interest in the economic development of Germany's overseas possessions. First, there were a number of British financial houses which had far longer experience than their German rivals of making investments in undeveloped territories. In the nineteenth century the export of British capital had played an important part in the opening up of economically backward regions. German colonies presented problems with which British investors were not unfamiliar.

Secondly, in the sixties and seventies of the nineteenth century British traders and financiers had been active in various territories which eventually came under German rule. In South West Africa English traders had exploited the guano deposits on the small islands off Angra Pequeña (Lüderitz Bay). Britain annexed these islands in 1867. The whaling harbour of Walfish Bay was annexed in 1878 and was administered by Cape Colony after 1884. In the sixties De Pass, Spence and Co. acquired from a native chief mining rights on the coast. The firm attempted to extract silver from the Pomana mine, near Walfish Bay.[10] It claimed to have spent £300,000 in South West Africa, and it made vigorous protests when Adolf Lüderitz of Bremen secured from the natives land to which it claimed prior rights. Traders and hunters from Cape Colony were active in South West Africa in the sixties and seventies.

In East Africa British commercial activities were ably fostered in the seventies and eighties by Sir John Kirk (Consul-General and Political Agent at Zanzibar) who wielded considerable influence over Said Bargash (Sultan of Zanzibar). British missionaries and explorers were beginning to open up the East African hinterland. In 1877-8 the Glasgow shipowner (Sir) William Mackinnon secured from Said Bargash a lease of territory on the mainland opposite Zanzibar, but the British Government refused to sanction the arrangement. At the same time the African Lakes Company was building steamers for use on the Zambezi, the Shire and Lake Nyasa. In 1884 (Sir) Harry Johnston secured land concessions on the southern side of Mount Kilimanjaro and at Taveta which he made over to the Manchester Chamber of Commerce.

On the West African coast British shipping and trading interests were far older than those of the Germans. In 1881, despite the recent rapid progress of German commerce in West Africa, the British trade in that region was still four times as great as the German. In the Cameroons alone, however, there were in 1885 nineteen German trading stations as against eleven British.

In the Pacific Britain had commercial interests in territories which eventually fell under German rule. In Samoa, for example, there were 138 British residents as against 145 German residents in 1884.

Germany's colonial tariff policy encouraged foreigners to trade in the colonies of the Reich. There was no attempt to secure for the mother country a monopoly of colonial trade by means of tariff preferences. German and foreign merchants paid the same rate of duties.[11] But certain German shipping companies serving the overseas possessions were subsidized and sometimes materials for railway construction in the colonies were drawn exclusively from Germany.

Three types of British capital investment and economic activity in the German colonies may be distinguished. First, there were British commercial undertakings which were established in the colonies before the eighties and survived after the territories came under German rule. These were mainly trading activities on the coasts of the colonies. Secondly, there were British plantation and mining enterprises which were started in the interior when the Germans had established law and order. In South West Africa there were British land and mining companies which were attracted to the territory by the grant of substantial privileges by the German Government. Thirdly, there were British enterprises which were established to work in (or for) British colonies but which incidentally did business also in German colonies. The shipping companies which handled the trade of Britain's possessions in Africa sometimes called at the ports of German colonies. The Uganda Railway was intended to open up British East Africa (Kenya), but it also brought to the coast products of the northern parts of German East Africa.

British commercial interests on the Cameroons coast had developed long before the German occupation of that territory and they were to some extent maintained. Britain's trade with the Cameroons was larger than her commerce with any other German colony. In 1895, eleven years after the German annexation, only nine firms traded at Duala, which was then the only commercial centre of any significance. Seven of these were British. But the two German firms (Woermann, and Jantzen & Thormählen) dominated the trade of the port.[12] Three years later German firms in the Cameroons numbered eleven and British eight.[13] At the same time British shipping was of greater importance than German shipping to the Cameroons. In 1897-8 fifty-one British steamers visited the colony as against twenty-nine German.

When the southern Cameroons began to be exploited and Kribi became the colony's second port British merchants established themselves there. Its main export was native rubber, which by 1914 was the most valuable product of the Cameroons. In 1911 branches of the two Liverpool firms (John Holt and Co. Ltd. and Hatton and Cookson Ltd.) and one Bristol firm (R. and W. King) were members of the Chamber of Commerce for the southern Cameroons.[14] European rubber plantations were established to supplement supplies of wild rubber collected by natives. The Nyong Rubber Plantation Co.[15] and the firm of John Holt set up rubber plantations.

There was some British commercial activity in the northern part of the Cameroons as well as on the coast. Adamaua, once a single trading area with its commercial centre at Yola, was now divided between Nigeria and the Cameroons. Haussa merchants were encouraged by the British to bring the products of German Adamaua to Yola and by the Germans to bring them to Garua. The value of the commerce of Garua amounted to £50,000 in 1913. But the Niger Co. acquired the only German trading factory at Garua (1911) and also maintained a trading station at Ngaundere.[16] Moreover, many goods were smuggled from German Adamaua to Nigeria.[17] The Germans replied by encouraging native merchants to bring goods from the northern Cameroons to the coast, and in 1902 a Haussa caravan brought ivory from Banjo overland to Victoria.

In the Cross River area, too, the Anglo-German frontier cut across old-established trading routes. The commercial centre of the Bamenda and Ossidinge districts was at Bali from which goods went down the Cross River to Calabar. Bali lay in the Cameroons and Calabar lay in Nigeria. A number of British firms at Calabar had trading stations in neighbouring regions in the Cameroons. John Holt (Liverpool) had five stations in the Ossidinge district in 1907. To meet British competition the North West Cameroons Company maintained several small steamers on the Cross River so as to trade on this waterway with the Cameroons. Attempts were made to bring goods from Bali to the coast at Rio del Rey which lay on the German side of the frontier. The trade of this harbour, however, amounted to only £31,783 in 1910.

In 1905 British firms had 134 trading stations in the Cameroons and John Holt maintained nearly fifty of them.[18] The British share in the colony's trade declined somewhat in the early years of the twentieth century.[19] This was partly because materials for building railways were imported only from Germany. And by 1914 British shipping had lost the leading position that it had once held in the territory.

In Togoland British commercial enterprise was confined largely to the Volta region. This river was the frontier between Togoland and the Gold Coast, but the channel itself as well as the whole of the estuary was in British hands. The frontier crossed old-established routes, and between 1894 and 1904 a customs union was maintained between Togoland and British territory lying on the left side of the lower Volta. British merchants benefited from this arrangement since they continued to trade with the German hinterland without paying customs duties. The British had better landing facilities at Ada and Keta than the Germans possessed at Lome and Anecho (Little Popo). The Germans tried to attract trade to Lome by building an iron pier there (1904).[20] But large ships could not reach the pier and goods had to be transferred to it by surf boats. To keep the commerce of the colony in their own hands the Germans founded the S.W. Africa Bank (1905), built railways from Lome to Palime (1907) and Atakpame (1913), and developed the trade of Kete Krachi on the River Volta. Of a dozen firms engaged in the export trade in 1910 only one (the house of Swanzy) was British. Two British shipping lines shared in the transport of Togoland's overseas commerce. The value of Togoland's trade with Britain in 1910 was £100,000.[21]

British economic activity in South West Africa was different from that in the Cameroons and in Togoland. In West Africa British merchants and shippers were interested in trade in tropical products secured from the natives, and there were also some British rubber plantations. In South West Africa, however, British enterprise helped to develop the colony by investments in land and in mining companies.[22]

The South West Africa Co. Ltd. was founded in London in 1892 by some Hamburg financiers headed by Dr. Scharlach and Herr

Wichmann, who were unable to raise money for their venture in Germany. It had British and German shareholders and directors. The company's capital of £300,000 was later raised to £2,000,000. The company secured from the German Government the exclusive right to exploit the minerals of the Otavi region; the grant of 13,000 sq. km. of land; and the sole right, for ten years, to build and operate a railway from the coast to certain districts in the interior. Owing to native risings and other difficulties little success attended the company's early mining and farming operations.

When the cattle plague of 1897 caused a breakdown in transport between Swakopmund and the hinterland, and the German Government built the Swakopmund-Windhoek railway, the Government proposed to use mule traction so as not to infringe the privileges of the South West Africa Co. Eventually the company surrendered its rights to operate the railway in return for new mining privileges in Amboland (1898).

In 1899 the South West Africa Co., in association with a big Berlin bank (the Discount Company) and the Exploration Co. Ltd. (London), established the Otavi Mining and Railway Company to exploit the Otavi mines and to link them by rail to the coast. In 1903 the South West Africa Co. handed over some of its privileges to the Otavi Co., in which it invested £400,000. The Otavi Co. increased its capital to £1,000,000. The Anglo-German Otavi Co. built a railway from Swakopmund to Tsumeb (1903-6) and the South West Africa Co. then extended the line to the Grootfontein farming region (1908). The line was bought by the German Government in 1910 but continued to be operated by the Otavi Co.

The Otavi Co. mined copper at Tsumeb, Asis, Guchab and Gross-Otavi. In 1913 production amounted to 44,500 tons. The exploitation of other mines in the district was left to a subsidiary company (the Otavi Exploring Syndicate Ltd.) which had found new deposits of copper and zinc when the war of 1914 interrupted its operations. Having handed over its mining and railway interests to the Otavi Co., the South West Africa Co. devoted itself to promoting farming and settlement. Between 1909 and 1914 it sold over 150,000 hectares of farm land.

The South West Africa Co. was connected with other enterprises in the colony, such as the *Hanseatische Land-, Minen- und Handels-gesellschaft* (of Hamburg) and the *Kaoko Land- und Minen-Gesell-schaft*. These companies failed to promote settlement or to work minerals, but their expeditions secured information which was subsequently of value in opening up parts of the territory.

In 1909 the South West Africa Co. had assets of over £1,000,000 and was reported to have spent £150,000 in opening up the territory in which it worked. The company and its main offshoot (the Otavi Co.) were the only privileged companies in South West Africa with adequate capital resources for the tasks that they undertook. The second privileged British company in this colony was the South African Territories Co. Ltd., which was established in 1895. It took over the assets and obligations of the Kharaskhoma Exploring and Prospecting Syndicate Ltd., which had in 1890 secured mining rights and land from native chiefs in the south-east of South West Africa. The German Government refused to recognize these privileges, but in 1892 the German Colonial Company for S.W. Africa granted by the syndicate land for 512 farms on condition that it built a railway from Lüderitz Bay to Aus. Since the company did not build a railway it secured land for only 128 farms. By May 1913 the company had sold 257,000 hectares and had leased another 589,000 hectares. In 1909 the company had assets of £29,238 and claimed that it had spent over £9,400 on expeditions. By 1914 the majority of its shares were in German hands.

Although the two British privileged companies in South West Africa brought few profits to their shareholders and had to face many disappointments they, and their Anglo-German daughter companies, helped to open up the colony by sending out expeditions and by settling farmers on the land. The exploitation of the Tsumeb copper mines, the construction of the Otavi Railway and the maintenance of two experimental farm institutes were achievements of real significance to the early development of a colony which lacked natural resources and suffered from serious native risings.

The exploitation of the guano resources of South West Africa was mainly in British hands. Until 1903 guano was an important export of the colony.[13] British capital also played some part in the first diamond rush in South West Africa. The Colmanskop Mines Ltd. of Cape Town (1908), which had a capital of £125,000, was one of the earliest diamond mining firms in the colony. In 1909 its production amounted to 123,854 carats, over one-fifth of the diamond output of South West Africa. The company declared a dividend of 55 per cent. after its first year's work. About half of the shares were in German hands.[14]

In the early years of the German occupation of South West Africa the British port of Walfish Bay, a tiny enclave (except for the coast) in German territory, was of some economic importance to the German colony. It was the best harbour on a thousand miles stretch of coast, and in 1884-93 it handled most of the limited trade of South West Africa. From this natural outlet for the sea-borne commerce of the colony a route (the *Baiweg*) crossed the Namib desert to the hinterland. A ship from Cape Town called at Walfish Bay about once a month. Some British capital was invested in this commerce. But the Germans eventually turned the adjacent open roadstead of Swakopmund into the main harbour of South West Africa. A mole was built there in 1899-1903. In the nineties a German steamer began to ply between Swakopmund and Cape Town. After 1893 Swakopmund made progress while the economic importance of Walfish Bay declined. The exports of South West Africa handled by Walfish Bay dropped in value from £9,500 in 1890 to £500 in 1903.[25]

In German East Africa British capital and mercantile enterprise played an indirect rather than a direct part in the colony's economic development. There had been for some time before the founding of the German colony a lively British trade on the East African coast. This commerce was centred at Zanzibar, which became a British Protectorate in 1890. Owing to its favourable location, its natural advantages as a harbour and its old-established trading connexions, this port continued to be the principal centre for the entrepôt trade of British and German territories on the adjacent mainland. British and Anglo-Indian capital and British shipping were active in this commerce. In 1910 about a third of the commerce of German East Africa was still handled by the port of Zanzibar.

Mombasa was of economic significance to German East Africa when the Uganda Railway to Kisumu (Port Florence) was built. A German railway expert declared that but for this railway the economic development of Muansa and Bukoba would have been delayed.[26] The agricultural products of this region, instead of going to the coast by caravan, could now be shipped across the Victoria Nyanza and could then go by rail to Mombasa.[27] The value of the trade of German harbours on the Victoria Nyanza rose from £22,569 in 1903 to £494,381 in 1910.[28] For a time some of Usambara's exports went by road from Taveta to Voi and then by the Uganda Railway to Mombasa.[29] In 1910, however, the Usambara Railway, serving the German port of Tanga, was extended from Mombo to New Moshi, and the Germans diverted to this line most of the traffic which had used the Taveta-Voi-Mombasa route.[30]

Although Zanzibar and Mombasa were in 1914 still of considerable significance as the channels through which some of the trade of German East Africa flowed, the Germans had tried to develop

Dar-es-Salaam as a commercial rival to Zanzibar and to establish firms of their own at Mombasa. As early as the year 1904 Sir Charles Eliot stated that 'the Germans are making a great effort to secure commercial preponderance on the East African coast, including Zanzibar' and that 'they are likely to succeed unless our merchants show more energy and enterprise than they have done in the last few years'. He added that in 1903-4 about half of the trade of British East Africa (Kenya) was carried in foreign, mainly German, vessels.[31]

There was for some years little British economic activity in German East Africa, although Indian traders and moneylenders flourished on the coast and some Boer farmers had established themselves in the colony. Until 1910 British capital appears to have shown little interest in plantations in the territory. In the rubber boom of that year, however, some companies were formed in London with a nominal capital of nearly £1,000,000 with the object of growing rubber and other tropical products on some twenty plantations.[32]

In Germany's possessions in the Pacific both commerce and the running of plantations was to a great extent in the hands of German companies. But some British, Australian and New Zealand firms were active in German as well as other colonies in the Pacific. In German Samoa, for example, three British plantation companies were established in 1909-10 to produce rubber, cocoa and coconuts.[33] One of them (Moors Samoan Trading and Plantations Ltd.) also engaged in general trade and maintained stations for that purpose. On Bougainville Island (in the German Solomons) the New Britain Trading and Planting Company maintained plantations.

Some Sydney trading companies, of which Burns, Philip and Co. was the most important, were engaged in commerce in Samoa and elsewhere in the South Seas. The rivalry between Burns, Philip and Co. and the Jaluit Company for the copra trade in the Marshall Islands involved the German and British governments in a long-drawn-out dispute (1904-6). The Jaluit Company was the only chartered colonial company whose administrative functions survived for more than a few years after the establishment of the German empire overseas. The officials of the company on the Marshall Islands used their administrative powers for commercial ends. Burns, Philip and Co. protested against the high export duty on copra, and the dispute ended when the German company lost its administrative functions and Burns, Philip and Co. got £4,100 compensation.[34]

On Nauru Island a British company (the Pacific Phosphate Co.

of London) exploited rich phosphate deposits after 1906. Some shares of the company were in the hands of the Jaluit Company, which held the original concession to work the phosphate resources. The Pacific Phosphate Co. employed 60 Europeans, 650 natives from the Caroline Islands and 100 Chinese. In May 1907 the first 4,000 tons of phosphate from Nauru reached Stettin. In 1913 the island's phosphate exports amounted to 138,725 tons.

Although the bulk of the traffic between the Reich and its colonies was in 1914 in the hands of German shipping companies, certain British lines also served some of the chief ports in the German colonial empire. The Union Castle line maintained several services to Africa, one of which touched at Dar-es-Salaam once a fortnight. The African Steamship Co. (Elder Dempster), in co-operation with the British and African Steam Navigation Co. Ltd., ran a weekly service between Liverpool and the principal harbours of West Africa including Duala and Kribi. The British American Steam Navigation Co. (Houston line) ran a steamer every three weeks between Cape Town and Lüderitz Bay. In the early years of the German occupation of Kiao Chow the trade of the port of Tsingtau was limited because, as Albert Ballin wrote, 'the landing facilities are hopelessly inadequate'.[35] At the beginning of the twentieth century there was no direct trade with Europe. Exports and imports had to be transhipped at Shanghai. Some of the trade between Tsingtau and Shanghai at this time was in the hands of British companies such as Jardine, Matheson and Co. and Butterfield and Swire. In March 1904 the first mole was opened to traffic at Tsingtau and in 1908 the P. and O. Steam Navigation Co. established a direct link between Kiao Chow and Europe. The Blue Funnel Line and Rickmer's Line also engaged in direct trade with Kiao Chow. In 1911 over a third (35 per cent.) of Kiao Chow trade was carried in British ships. Between 1900 and 1913 the number of British ships entering Kiao Chow rose from 39 to 214. The German colony which depended most upon British shipping was Samoa. In 1910 no less than 91 out of 94 steamships entering the harbours of Samoa were British.[36]

Communication by submarine cable between Germany and her overseas possessions was in 1914 largely in the hands of British companies. East Africa and South West Africa were entirely dependent upon British cables. The Eastern and South Africa Telegraph Co. maintained a cable between Dar-es-Salaam, Bagamojo and Zanzibar and connected Swakopmund with its Cape Town-Mossamedes (Angola) cable, and so linked both East and South West Africa with the world's cable network. Tsingtau (Kiao Chow) had German cables to Chefoo and to Shanghai. But from Shanghai lines maintained by foreign firms[37] had to be used for communication with Germany. For twenty years cable communication between the Cameroons and Germany used a British line from Duala to Bonny (Nigeria). Only in 1913 did a Cologne firm complete a cable which brought both Togoland and the Cameroons into direct contact with Berlin by a line under German control.[38]

One overland telegraph line in the German colonies was in British hands. This was in East Africa. It was constructed in 1902-3 from Abercorn (Rhodesia) to Bismarckburg and Ujiji (on Lake Tanganyika in German East Africa).[39] The line belonged to the African Transcontinental Telegraph Co. which was founded by Cecil Rhodes in 1892 to build a telegraph from Cape Town to Cairo. Since there was at the beginning of the twentieth century no German telegraph across East Africa from Dar-es-Salaam to Lake Tanganyika the British line was of considerable benefit to the Germans. By using this line in conjunction with the submarine cable to Zanzibar and Cape Town it was possible to communicate directly from Dar-es-Salaam to Bismarckburg and Ujiji. The telegraph was particularly valuable to the German authorities during the native revolts in the southern parts of East Africa in 1905-7. During the military operations in German East Africa in 1914-16 the telegraph between Abercorn and Bismarckburg remained in operation. The English postmaster at Abercorn and the German postmaster at Bismarckburg continued to exchange daily test signals. It may be added that in 1914 the northern and north-western parts of the Cameroons still depended largely upon the Nigerian system of telegraphs for contact with the outside world.

German newspapers in the colonies were almost entirely dependent for their news from the outside world upon Reuter, the British news agency. Reuter, Havas and Wolff divided the world into regions each of which was exclusively served by one of the three agencies. And the German colonies fell in Reuter's area. Occasionally it was possible to arrange for Wolff (the German agency) to supply some items of news and the *Deutsch-Ostafrikanische Zeitung* tried to build up its own news service from Germany but, on the whole, little success attended the efforts to break Reuter's monopoly.[40]

In relation to Britain's total capital exports and to her world-wide economic interests her contribution to the development of Germany's overseas possessions in the years 1884-1914 was a trifling matter. But the crumbs that the British investor bestowed upon those territories were of real significance in assisting them at a time

69

when Germans themselves were singularly reluctant to put money into their own colonies. British financiers, investors, traders, planters and shipowners did their most important work in the German colonies in the first twenty years or so of their existence. It was only in the years immediately preceding the outbreak of war in 1914 that Germany took a more active interest than before in the exploitations of the colonies.

REFERENCES

1. H. Feis, *Europe, the World's Banker*, 1870-1914 (Yale University Press, 1930), p. 74.
2. German investments in Johannesburg in 1896 were estimated at £25,000,000 (Hatzfeldt to the German Foreign Office, 4 January, 1896, in E. T. S. Dugdale, *German Diplomatic Documents*, 1871-1914 (1929), II, p. 388).
3. F. Baltzer, *Die Kolonialbahnen* . . . (1916), p. 71.
4. See various propaganda speeches by Dr. Bernhard Derburg: *Zielpunkte des deutschen Kolonialwesens* (two lectures, Berlin, 1907); *Koloniale Finanzprobleme* (Berlin, 1907); *Koloniale Lehrjahre* (Stuttgart, 1907); *Südwestafrikanische Eindrücke* and *Industrielle Fortschritte in den Kolonien* (two lectures, Berlin, 1909).
5. This refers to Tanganyika Territory (German East Africa without Ruanda-Urundi): see C. Gillman, 'A population map of Tanganyika Territory', Appendix IX of the *Report . . . to the Council of the League of Nations on . . . Tanganyika Territory . . .*, 1935 (1936).
6. i.e. companies registered under English law (*Deutsches Kolonial-Lexikon*, Leipzig, III, p. 63).
7. In 1903 cattle exports to Cape Colony represented two-thirds of South West Africa's exports.
8. See tables in Part II of the official report, *Die deutschen Schutzgebiete . . .*, 1910-11 (Berlin, 1912). British trade with Germany's colonies was much smaller than German trade with British dominions and colonies.
9. G. L. Beer, *African Questions at the Paris Peace Conference* (1923), p. 20.
10. When German authority was established in South West Africa the exclusive right of the British firm to exploit the Pomana Mine was recognized (1886). The firm made no use of this right. When diamonds were discovered in South West Africa in 1908 it was established that these stones existed in the Pomana district. In 1912 Daniel De Pass and Co. (successor of De Pass, Spence and Co.) sold its rights to the mine and adjacent land to a German company.
11. The principle that there should be no tariff preferences for German goods imported into German colonies rested to a great extent upon international agreements; the Final Act of the Berlin West Africa (Congo) Conference for the south-east corner of the Old Cameroons, most of the New Cameroons and all German East Africa; an Anglo-German agreement of 1886 for the islands in the Western Pacific, and the Samoa Treaty of 1890 for that colony.
12. T. Seitz, *Vom Aufstieg und Niederbruch deutscher Kolonialmacht*, I, 'Aus dem alten Kamerun' (Karlsruhe, 1927), p. 87. It has been pointed out that Woermann's 'great commercial success on the Cameroons was due in large

part to his willingness to give greater amounts of credit to natives than other traders' (H. R. Rudin, *The Germans in the Cameroons, 1884-1914* (1938), p. 226).

13. S. Passarge, 'Kamerun' (in Hans Meyer, *Das deutsche Kolonialreich* (Leipzig, 1909), I, p. 532).

14. *Die Handel in Südkamerun in den Jahren 1908 bis 1911* (Report of the Chamber of Commerce for the southern Cameroons, Berlin, 1912): list of firms on pp. 1-2.

15. The company was established in London in 1911 with a nominal capital of £150,000.

16. H. R. Rudin, ch. 6 and article on 'Garua' in the *Deutsches Kolonial-Lexikon*, I, p. 679. In 1914 it was reported that a German shipping company was to be formed to establish communication from Garua to the sea through British territory by way of the Niger-Benue waterway system.

17. *Die deutschen Schutzgebiete in Afrika und der Südsee, 1910-11* (Official Report of the German Colonial Office, 1912), p. 63.

18. André Chéradame, *La Colonisation et les Colonies allemandes* (Paris, 1905), p. 346.

19. Although the general tendency was for German trade to develop more rapidly than British trade in the Cameroons in the early twentieth century there were years in which the opposite was true. According to the official report of the German Colonial Office for 1910 British trade had made more progress than German trade in that year in the Cameroons (p. 73).

20. The pier was seriously damaged by high seas in 1911 and was rebuilt.

21. British exporters might have secured a larger share of the trade with the natives not only in Togoland but in West Africa generally if they had sent out cheaper goods. Consul-General Braithwaite-Wallis pointed out in 1910 that in Togoland 'British exporters often make the mistake of sending out manufactured products of too good a quality. German manufacturers can produce an article almost identical in appearance, cheaper in price, although not so good nor so lasting as the British sample. The native buyer will nearly always select the cheaper article, seldom appreciating or realising the difference in quality.' The Consul added that in Togoland 'there is no preference and British merchants are treated with consideration by the Government' (*Report on the Trade of Togoland*, Cmd. 4962 of 1910).

22. See *Denkschrift über die im südwestafrikanischen Schutzgebiete tätigen Land- und Minengesellschaften* (No. 683 of the *Reichstagsdrucksachen*, II. *Legis- laturperiode, I. Session, 1903-5); Schlussbericht der Kommission zur Prüfung der Rechte und Pflichten und der bisherigen Tätigkeit der Land- und Bergwerks- gesellschaften in Südwestafrika* (No. 193 of the *Reichstagsdrucksachen*, XX. *Legislaturperiode, 2. Session, 1909-10*: particularly Appendix 9 by Prof. Anton); H. Jäckel, *Die Landesgesellschaften in den deutschen Schutzgebiete* (1909); T. Leutwein, *Elf Jahre Gouverneur in Deutsch-Südwestafrika* (1907), ch. 11; J. K. Vietor, *Kolonialpolitik und Bodenreform* (1912); L. Sander, *Geschichte der deutschen Kolonialgesellschaft für Südwestafrika* (2 vols., Berlin, 1912); and S. H. Frankel, *Capital Investment in Africa* (1938), pp. 218-19.

23. Otto Mayer, *Die Entwicklung der Handelsbeziehungen Deutschlands zu seinen Kolonien* (Munich, 1913), p. 85.

24. See *Deutsch Süd-West-Afrika: Denkschrift betreffend die Verhältnisse im Diamentengebiet* (petition to the Reichstag of six members of the Local Council (*Bezirksrat*) of Lüderitz Bay, April 1910).

25. See articles in the *Deutsches Kolonial-Lexikon* on 'Baiweg' (1,118), 'Walfisch-bai' (III, 663) and 'Swakopmund' (III, 44); T. Leutwein, *Elf Jahre Gouverneur in Deutsch-Südwestafrika* (Berlin, 1907), pp. 132-40; Dr. Dove, 'Deutsch-Südwestafrika' (in *Deutschland und seine Kolonien in Jahre 1896* (Berlin, 1897, p. 163); and Otto Mayer, *Die Entwicklung der Handelsbeziehungen Deutschlands zu seinen Kolonien* (Munich, 1913).

26. F. Baltzer, *Die Kolonialbahnen* . . . (Berlin and Leipzig, 1916), p. 154. Baltzer wrote: 'We can only greet with satisfaction (the fact) that England has opened up the Victoria Nyanza for us by her railway and has fixed reasonably low (transport) charges.' Graf von Götzen (Governor of German East Africa, 1901-6), after visiting the Victoria Nyanza region in the summer of 1905, wrote: 'I saw the beneficial influence which the British Uganda Railway was beginning to have upon our stations on the Lake, and in association with my local officials, I was able to make arrangements for us to draw every possible commercial and military advantage from this factor.' (*Deutsch-Ostafrika im Aufstand, 1905-6* (Berlin, 1909), p. 2.)

27. Sir Charles Eliot, *The East Africa Protectorate* (1905), p. 221.

28. *Die deutschen Schutzgebiete in Afrika und der Südsee, 1910-11* (annual report of the German Colonial Office, 1912), p. 38. The Uganda Railway was also used to send postal matter to parts of German East Africa.

29. Most, 'Die wirtschaftliche Entwicklung Deutsch-Ostafrikas 1885-1905' (in the *Jahresbericht der Klosterschule Rossleben*, 1906, p. 24).

30. The Usambara and Uganda railways were eventually joined by the Voi-New Moshi line in April 1916. The line was built on the eve of General Smuts's offensive against German East Africa and was of military—not economic—significance.

31. Sir Charles Eliot, op. cit., pp. 228-9.

32. The companies were: East Africa Rubber Plantations Co. Ltd. (1909); Manihot Rubber Plantations Ltd.; Muhesa Rubber Plantations Ltd.; Mombo Rubber Plantation Ltd.; Lewa Rubber Estates Ltd.; Kamna Rubber Estate Ltd.; and Kifulu Rubber Estates Ltd. (all 1910).
   The Lewa Rubber Estates Ltd. took over the Lewa Plantation of the *Deutsch-Ostafrikanische Plantagengesellschaft AG*. The Vice-President of the Reichstag called this plantation the *Schmerzenskind* of all the big planta-tions in East Africa (Hermann Paasche, *Deutsch Ostafrika* (1906), p. 197). The German company had been founded in 1886 and was the first plantation company in German East Africa. It had grown first tobacco and then coffee without success before turning in 1903 to the cultivation of rubber. In 1910 the *Deutsch-Ostafrikanische Plantagengesellschaft* was in financial difficulties and was glad to sell the Lewa plantation to the Lewa Rubber Estates Ltd.
   A. F. Calvert stated in *German East Africa* (1917) that by 1914 over £2,000,000 of British capital had been invested in the Usambara plantation region of East Africa (pp. 30-1).

33. Papaseca Plantations Ltd. (Sydney, 1909), capital £30,000; Upolu Rubber and Cocoa Estates Ltd. (London, 1910), capital £90,000; and Moors Samoan Trading and Plantations Ltd. (1910), capital £60,000.

34. Alfred Zimmermann, *Geschichte der deutschen Kolonialpolitik* (Berlin, 1914), pp. 282-3.

35. Letter from Albert Ballin (19 March, 1901) quoted in B. Huldermann, *Albert Ballin* (London, 1922), p. 97.

36. The Union Steamship Co. of New Zealand and the Australian Mail Co. played an important part in Samoa in handling the overseas trade, the passenger traffic and the carriage of postal matter.

37. e.g. the Eastern Extension Australasia and China Telegraph Co. But a German-Dutch company maintained cables from Wusung (by Shanghai) to Tomil (on Yap Island in the Carolines), Menado (in the Dutch island of Celebes) and Guam (American possession).

38. This cable ran from Emden in Germany to Teneriffe (Canary Islands), Monrovia (Liberia) and Pernambuco.

39. Ujiji is near Kigoma, the terminus (1914) of the trans-continental railway from Dar-es-Salaam.

40. D. Redeker, *Journalismus in Deutsch-Ostafrika, 1899-1916* (Frankfurt-am-Main, 1937), pp. 127-9.

Chapter VI

GERMAN ECONOMIC PENETRATION
IN THE MIDDLE EAST, 1870-1914

THERE has been a tendency for those who study the policy of the Germany of Wilhelm II in the Middle East to concentrate their attention unduly upon the Berlin-Baghdad Railway scheme. It is true that this grandiose project was of great significance not only from an economic point of view but also because it symbolized Germany's far-reaching political and territorial ambitions in Asiatic Turkey. But Germany's economic penetration of parts of the Middle East involved far more than the construction of a railway to Baghdad. This famous line engaged the attention of diplomats, and so accounts of the negotiations concerning the project appear in political histories. Other factors, however, deserve examination if the significance of Germany's economic penetration of the Middle East in 1870-1914 is to be appreciated. Irrigation and other public works, farming, trade, cotton, oil and settlement come into the picture as well as railways.

In the years immediately following the establishment of a united Reich in 1871 German manufacturers made rapid progress and German industrialists and financiers sought new overseas markets and fresh sources of raw materials. Germany was late in the field, and the colonies that Bismarck secured in the eighties had only limited possibilities from the economic point of view. In the circumstances it was not unnatural that Germany should turn her attention to the Middle East.

There was another factor in the situation. The middle years of the nineteenth century had seen in Germany a struggle between those who favoured the establishment of a Greater Reich (to include the German-speaking subjects of Austria) and a Lesser Reich. Bismarck had founded a Lesser Reich. There were extremists who hoped to gain in the economic field what had been lost in the political struggle. They dreamed of a powerful industrialized Germany which would, from an economic point of view, dominate all Central Europe and the Balkans. They hoped to secure the support of Germans living in Austria-Hungary and the Balkans. And if a

74

German *Mitteleuropa* were established then a new vista appeared to the extreme Pan-Germans—the dream of 'a real territorial empire, founded on a coherent chain of German settlements along the Danube and perhaps along the German-built railway through Asia Minor . . .'.[1]

The Middle East was a territory of about 4½ million square kilometres with an estimated population of 35 million.[2] It had formerly been of great significance both as a transit region and as a centre of agricultural production. In the ancient world the products of the farms, the forests and the mines of the Middle East had been of fundamental importance to the economy of the Mediterranean region. In the Middle Ages the caravan routes from the Persian Gulf to the ports of the Levant had carried much of the trade between Europe and the Far East. Owing to the domination of the Middle East by the Turks most of this trade had for centuries gone by sea round the Cape of Good Hope, though in the seventeenth century the English Levant Company (which had an important trading station at Aleppo) was still able to use the old land route. With the opening of the Suez Canal (1869), however, the Middle East again became of significance as a transit region.

Gross Turkish misgovernment and neglect had greatly restricted the economic productivity of the Middle East. In Syria and Palestine many of the terraces for the cultivation of the hillsides had long fallen into utter decay with the result that there had been much erosion.[3] In Mesopotamia virtually nothing was done to revive the ancient system of irrigation.[4]

Two things were required for the economic recovery of the Middle East—the introduction of European capital and technical skill combined with a genuine reform of the corrupt Turkish system of administration. If this were done progress might be expected in extending in Anatolia the production of wheat, wool, mohair, figs and nuts; the rearing of horses; the manufacture of carpets; and the mining of chrome, lead and copper. The rich timber and copper resources of the Taurus Mountains might be adequately exploited. Mesopotamia might rival Egypt as a centre of cotton production, while Syria, the Lebanon and Palestine might develop their production of grapes, oranges and other fruits.

As early as the forties of the nineteenth century there were Germans who drew attention to the economic possibilities of the Middle East. Von Moltke visited Constantinople in 1841 and advocated the establishment of German settlements in Palestine.[5] At the same time Friedrich List wrote: 'All the Continental Powers have . . . a common interest that neither of the two routes from the Mediterranean to the Red Sea and to the Persian Gulf should fall into the exclusive possession of England, nor remain impassable owing to Asiatic barbarism. To commit the duty of protecting these important points to Austria would ensure the best guarantee to all European nations.'[6]

There was, however, little German economic activity in the Mediterranean or in Asiatic Turkey in the middle years of the nineteenth century, though reference may be made to the far-reaching plans of Freiherr von Bruck (who played a leading part in founding the Austrian Lloyd shipping company at Trieste)[7] and to the settlement of some small 'Templer Colonies' in Palestine.[8]

Some years later Germans again showed a lively interest in the economic potentialities of the Middle East. Dr. Sprenger for example wrote a book called *Babylon—the richest land in Ancient Times*.[9] He claimed that 'Asia Minor is the only territory in the world which has not yet been monopolized by a Great Power. And yet it is the finest field for colonization. If Germany does not miss the opportunity and seizes it before the Cossacks grab it, she will have secured the best part in the division of the world.' Dr. Sprenger's views had some influence upon German public opinion in the eighties. Subsequent research showed that he had considerably exaggerated the area of Mesopotamia under cultivation in ancient times. In 1892 Carl Kaerger advocated the exploitation of Asia Minor which would be an ideal 'field for German colonization'[10] and in 1897 Carl Kannenberg drew attention to the mineral wealth of the same region.[11] At the same time the Pan-German League issued a pamphlet with the self-explanatory title, *Germany's Claims to the Turkish Inheritance*.[12]

There was little time to lose if Germany were to establish her influence in the Middle East, for in the eighties and nineties other countries were awakening to the possibility of exploiting the resources of the Ottoman Empire and neighbouring territories. Great Britain had many interests in the Middle East. British investors held about 29 per cent. of the Turkish Government debt in 1881. The British Government had in 1875 secured 176,000 shares in the Suez Canal Company. Cyprus was under British administration (1878). After Britain's victory at Tel el Kebir her Minister and Agent wielded great authority in Egypt. Great Britain had old well-established political and economic interests in the Persian Gulf and the Shatt el Arab where she tried to suppress slave-trading and gun-running. Messrs. Lynch Brothers ran a regular shipping service on the Tigris and Euphrates while for some years British commercial houses virtually monopolized Mesopotamia's trade. Commerce between Baghdad and Persia on the route running through Kermanshah was in British hands. Baron Reuter (a British subject) secured financial and mining concessions in Persia in the nineties. In the twentieth century, however, British interests in Turkey declined somewhat partly because—in the words of Sir Edward Grey—'a very poor set of financiers had got commercial enterprise in Turkey in their hands.'[13]

Russia, too, was showing an increasing interest in the Middle East. In 1878 she gained Kars and Batum while in the eighties she established her authority in the Transcaspian (Turcoman) District. Between 1888 and 1897 her trade with Persia increased in value from £2,000,000 to £3,500,000. From 1901 onwards the Russian Steam Navigation Company sent the *Kornilov* on a series of voyages from Odessa to the Persian Gulf and Bombay.

The French had well-established commercial interests in the Near East, particularly in Egypt and Syria. It was reported that in 1881 French investors held nearly 39 per cent. of the Turkish Government debt while in 1902 an official inquiry estimated that French investments in Asiatic Turkey amounted to 354 million francs.

In the eighties and nineties the Germans began to forge ahead in Turkey. In 1880-1 the virtual bankruptcy of the Turkish Government led to the establishment of the Ottoman Public Debt Administration on the Council of which the German bondholders had a representative.[14] In 1888 the *Deutsche Bank* arranged a loan for the Sultan after the *Banque Impériale Ottomane* had declined to do so. Shortly afterwards the *Deutsche Bank* not only secured important interests in Balkan railways (by acquiring shares in the *Betriebsgesellschaft für Orientalische Eisenbahnen*) but also played a leading part in the establishment of the Anatolian Railway Company (1889).[15] Next came an understanding with the *Banque Impériale Ottomane* for co-operation in financial operations in Turkey.[16] The German Levant Line opened up a direct shipping service between Hamburg and Constantinople. In the late nineties the commercial house of Wonckhaus began trading operations at Baghdad, Abadan and Bushire. The value of goods sent from Hamburg to Turkey rose from £66,000 in 1890 to £520,250 in 1898. The Turkish Government began to place contracts with Krupp of Essen for war materials.[17] Germany's commercial offensive achieved a considerable measure of success. German traders, supported by their consuls, vigorously pushed their wares and made every effort to meet the needs of new

77

customers. German goods might be of low quality but they were cheap.[18]

Military missions under Köhler (1880) and von der Goltz (1883)[19] reformed the Turkish army and gained considerable influence at Constantinople. In 1889 the young Kaiser paid his first visit to Abdul Hamid. In 1897 Marschall von Bieberstein took up his post as German Ambassador to the Porte. He was an able diplomat and successfully fostered German political and economic ambitions in the Ottoman Empire. Shortly after his arrival he wrote an optimistic report on Germany's trade prospects. He stated that there was 'plenty of scope for useful future expansion for solid enterprises, employing German capital and German industry. There are—quite apart from special services for the army—railways, ports and bridges to build, electrical works to erect for lighting, tramways, etc., and the really wretched condition of most of the steamers that ply regularly here offers good chances for German competition. We shall naturally not be left alone to do all this, and certain concessions will be granted to others. But one thing we must claim for ourselves, and that is the connecting up of the present sphere of interests of the Anatolian Railway with the river districts of the Tigris and Euphrates, and so on to the Persian Gulf.' Against the last sentence the Kaiser wrote in the margin: 'Without question.'[20]

In the autumn of 1898 the Kaiser went to Constantinople for the second time and also visited Damascus and Jerusalem.[21] The visit coincided with the granting to the Anatolian Railway Company of a concession at Haidar Pasha (by Scutari) which was to be the new terminus and the western port of the Berlin-Baghdad Railway. The harbour, built in 1899-1903, had a 600-metre breakwater with a lighthouse at either end. This was constructed parallel to the coast to protect the port from winter gales. Large quays, warehouses, granaries and cranes were provided. The imposing railway station— designed by Cuno and built by Holzman and Company—was opened in 1909. The new European quarter at Haidar Pasha soon had a population of 35,000. In 1912 the harbour was used by 166 steamships and 179 sailing vessels. A train-ferry at Haidar Pasha enabled passengers to travel in Asia by the same coach that they had used in Europe.

Meanwhile, progress was being made with the railway itself.[22] As soon as direct railway communication was established between Berlin and Constantinople (1888) a group of German banks—led by the *Deutsche Bank*—formed the Ottoman Railway Company of Anatolia. The Ankara-Eskisehir branch was completed in 1892, and the main line from Scutari to Konia²³ was opened shortly afterwards. Most of these lines were built by the Frankfurt firm of Holzmann and Company.

In 1902-3 the Company secured from the Ottoman Government a concession to extend the line to Baghdad and the Persian Gulf with a branch to Khanikin. A new company—the Imperial Ottoman Baghdad Railway Company—was established to build and run the new line.²⁴ German commercial and industrial interests seem to have taken an almost purely business view of the plan, but the Kaiser and some of his advisers regarded the scheme as a means of extending German political influence in Turkey.

Many difficulties delayed the project. Russia criticized the original route which was uncomfortably close to her own frontier, and the plan was consequently changed. By the Potsdam Agreement of 1909 Russia withdrew her objection to the construction of a branch of the Baghdad Railway to Khanikin near the Persian frontier. As early as 1899 the Government of India issued a warning that 'the obvious corollary to a system of German railways in Asia Minor would be similar railroads to the Persian border and through Mesopotamia to the Persian Gulf.'²⁵ In 1903 Lord Lansdowne announced that Great Britain would resist any attempt of a foreign Power to establish a fortified port on the Persian Gulf. And in 1905 the Committee of Imperial Defence declared that Britain 'should have a share in the control of the extension of the Baghdad Railway to the Persian Gulf with a view to ensuring the effective neutralization of the terminus.²⁶ Great Britain was also interested in maintaining her trade in Mesopotamia and in the development of cotton-growing in that territory. Sir William Willcocks had prepared for the Turkish Government a great irrigation scheme for Mesopotamia. The first instalment of the plan was the Hindiya Barrage. It was constructed by the firm of Sir John Jackson and was opened in 1913.²⁷ When the Royal Navy began to build oil-driven ships Great Britain naturally became interested in the oil-bearing districts of Mesopotamia and Persia and supported the Anglo-Persian Oil Company (in which it had large investments) against its German, Dutch and American rivals. By 1908 the leading promoters of the Baghdad Railway realized that foreign opposition was too strong for them. Helfferich admitted to von Gwinner that 'the dream of a Baghdad Railway—German to the Gulf—is over.'²⁸ It was, however, not until 1914 that Germany and Great Britain came to an agreement on the Baghdad Railway which safeguarded British political and economic interests in the region to be served by the last section of the railway from Baghdad to Basra.[29]

The continuation of the Baghdad Railway was also hindered by political unrest in Turkey—such as the fall of Abdul Hamid during the Young Turk revolution—and by financial difficulties. Insufficient capital was raised in Germany itself, and British financiers were reluctant to co-operate on the terms proposed by von Gwinner and his colleagues. Discussion between von Gwinner and Sir Ernest Cassel in 1909-10 had no immediate results.[30]

Despite these difficulties the Baghdad Railway reached Bulgurlu at the foot of the Taurus Mountains in 1904. This remained the terminus until 1911. Then construction was resumed and by 1914 the line reached Ras el Ain some 200 miles beyond Aleppo. In the last section of the line there were some gaps in the Taurus and Amanus Mountains where various tunnels were not ready. The Mediterranean ports of Mersina and Iskanderun (Alexandretta) were linked to the Baghdad Railway. The existing Mersina-Tarsus-Adana line was incorporated in the German-controlled railway system in 1906 while the Toprakkale-Iskanderun branch was opened in 1913. The Railway Company began to build new quays at Iskanderun. In Mesopotamia the Baghdad-Samarra section of the line was under construction in 1914. During the war of 1914-18 the Germans continued the main portion of the railway from Ras el Ain to El Helif and Nusaybin. A river port was constructed at Carablus where the line crossed the upper Euphrates.[31]

At the same time that the Germans were building the Baghdad Railway they were indirectly interested in another important Turkish line. This was the 1,126-mile narrow gauge Hejaz line which was constructed in 1900-8 by the Sultan and ran from Damascus to Medina. Ostensibly the building of the line had a twofold object. From an administrative and military point of view the line brought distant provinces into much closer touch with Constantinople than they had been previously. From a religious point of view the new line greatly facilitated pilgrimages and much of the money to build it was subscribed by faithful Moslems. But German engineers— such as Meissner Pasha—played a prominent part in building the line. The writers of the official British history of military operations in the Middle East in 1914-18 may well be correct when they write of this railway: 'The Sultan Abdul Hamid, whose dearest project it was, saw in it the consolidation of his authority; Germany looked forward to controlling through him Western Arabia, to threatening British communications in the Red Sea, to decreasing the political and military, and even (though to a much smaller extent) the economic, importance of the Suez Canal.'³² In 1914 German commercial influence was already dominant in Haifa which was eventually expected to develop into the Mediterranean terminus of the Hejaz Railway.³³

Although the Baghdad Railway was far from complete in 1914 it was already beginning to have significant economic results. The new port of Haidar Pasha handled six per cent. of Turkey's trade. In Adana (Cilicia) province in Anatolia 'the advent of the Baghdad Railway into remoter parts of the vilayet has had the effect of bringing large tracts of good arable land under the plough'.³⁴ The Levant Cotton Company fostered cotton-growing in this region. The principal offices, experimental gardens and factory of the firm were at Adana on the Baghdad Railway.³⁵ The activities of the Germans helped to increase the cotton production of Asiatic Turkey from 60,000 bales in 1904 to 92,000 bales in 1908. A German firm—subsidiary to the Baghdad Railway Company—secured in 1909 a concession to irrigate parts of the Konia Plain for wheat-growing. By 1912 a system of canals drawing water from Lake Beïschir (or Kiril Gör) was irrigating an area of 40,000 hectares. The possibility of growing cotton, wheat, maize, opium and tobacco in Mesopotamia also aroused Germany's interest,³⁶ and Germans gave financial support to the £26,000,000 irrigation scheme planned by Sir William Willcocks. By 1914 German engineers were boring for oil at Quaiyara (by Mosul) and German financiers had a share in the new Turkish Petroleum Company.

German ships served many ports in the Middle East. The Levant Line ran several services in these waters. The Hamburg-America line maintained a service to Basra and ran ships direct from the United States to Constantinople. German shipping passing through the Suez Canal rose from 2¼ million tons in 1907 to 3 million tons in 1912. Over forty German steamships used the harbours of Mersina, Tripoli (Syria) and Beirut in 1912. Over 200 ships passed through the Straits from the Mediterranean to the Black Sea and in the reverse direction in 1913. German banks—such as the *Deutsche Bank*, the *Deutsche Orientbank*³⁷ and the *Deutsche Palästina Bank*— played an increasingly important part in the economic life of the Middle East. When the Germans were temporarily out of favour at Constantinople owing to the fall of their friend Abdul Hamid the *Deutsche Bank* helped to restore good relations by granting the new Turkish Government a loan which had been refused by French financiers (1910). The Imperial German Post Office (*Reichspost*) had its own post-offices in Constantinople, Smyrna, Beirut, Jaffa and Jerusalem. German trading interests in Turkey were expanding. The German-owned share of the Turkish Government Debt rose from a mere 5 per cent. in 1881 to about 20 per cent. in 1914. In 1887 Turkey's imports from Germany amounted to 6 per cent.: in 1910 the figure was 21 per cent. The value of Germany's total trade with Turkey rose from £5,580,000 in 1908 to £8,620,000 in 1913. Textile exports to Turkey alone amounted to £1,400,000 in 1911-12.[38]

Military influence in Turkey went hand in hand with commercial influence. In 1913 General Otto Liman von Sanders—the future defender of the Dardanelles—was appointed head of the Turkish army corps in Constantinople. In the same year Germany was discussing with her allies of the Triple Alliance a possible division of the Ottoman Empire in the event of that state collapsing. 'Germany meant to reserve to herself the central portion of Asia Minor, Aleppo and northern Mesopotamia, as well as the harbours of Alexandretta (Iskanderun), Mersina and Adana.'[39]

Germany's economic interests in Persia though far smaller than those in Turkey were not without significance. Great Britain and Russia had older and more substantial interests in Persia than Germany, and these two powers came to an agreement in 1907 on spheres of influence. There was a central neutral zone in Persia which lay between the Russian zone in the north and the British zone in the south-east. By the Potsdam Agreement in 1909 Germany renounced her claims to commercial concessions in the Russian zone. Russia agreed to the construction of the Khanikin branch of the Baghdad Railway. The extension of this proposed line to Tehran was to be built by Russian concessionaires.[40] Germany may well have hoped to strengthen her commercial position in the neutral zone. In 1909 Wassmuss was appointed German Consul to the Persian Gulf. During his first short stay—he left in 1910—his forceful assertion of Germany's rights caused some concern to Major Percy Cox, the British Consul General at Bushire.

At this time it was stated that considerable quantities of German goods (under the guise of Russian goods) were being imported into western Persia. In 1910 the British Ambassador in Berlin was told that Germany demanded in Persia 'the Open Door and a fair field for German capitalists and exporters.'[41] In the years before the war of 1914-18 the Germans were actively promoting a scheme to irrigate the Karun valley. A branch of the *Deutsche Orientbank* was opened at Tehran. Cultural relations were fostered by the establishment of a German College (1907). Germany's exports to

Persia increased from £110,000 in 1908 to £406,500 in 1911. In the same period her imports from Persia rose from £10,000 to £55,000. The ground was being prepared for the Wassmuss mission to Persia which did some mischief to the Allied cause during the War of 1914-18.[42]

REFERENCES

1. A. Mendelssohn-Bartholdy, *The War and German Society* (New Haven: Yale University Press, 1937), p. 206 n.
2. i.e. Asiatic Turkey, Egypt and Persia.
3. W. C. Lowdermilk states that in 1850 the population of Palestine was under 200,000. 'By the middle of the nineteenth century the conditions of the population and the land reached their lowest ebb. Insecurity prevailed and Bedouins plundered farms and robbed travellers and caravans on the road. Petty officials cruelly exploited the defenceless fellaheen. The grazing culture of the desert Arabs completely replaced the refined ancient agriculture. Herds of goats overran the country, leaving the land defenceless before run-off from the heavy winter rains which year after year eroded soils into the valleys and out to sea.' (*Palestine, Land of Promise* (1945), pp. 59-60.)
4. The Admiralty's Geographical Handbook on *Iraq and the Persian Gulf* (1944) observes: 'The common view that the ruin of the land [i.e. Mesopotamia] was effected in a few years by the destruction of irrigation head-works at the hands of Mongol invaders in the thirteenth or fourteenth centuries A.D. is certainly false. Some of the Euphrates canals were still in use in the early nineteenth century when Chesney sailed down the Saqlawiya—the Abbasid Nahr Isa—into the Tigris, but all had suffered from administrative neglect and from the gradual silting up of both main and branch canals over a period of centuries. It is relatively easy for local cultivators to maintain some head of water in their distributaries by their own efforts and at the expense of weaker neighbours, but when it becomes uneconomical to clear the silt from the canal bed because of the increasing height of the banks, a new channel can be cut alongside. But it needs a strong central government to co-ordinate these efforts, to ensure the economic use of water, and, above all, to develop new schemes necessitated by changes in the course of the rivers which supply the water' (pp. 433-4).
5. See quotations from von Moltke's writings in C. Andler, *Les Origines du Pangermanisme* (Paris, 1915), pp. 161-4.
6. F. List, *The National System of Political Economy*, 1841 (English trans. by S. S. Lloyd, 1928), p. 337.
7. See R. Charmatz, *Minister Freiherr von Bruck. Der Vorkämpfer Mitteleuropas* (Leipzig, 1916), for Bruck's activities and plans.
8. W. Mönckmeier, *Die deutsche überseeische Auswanderung* (Jena, 1912), pp. 225-6 and Davis Trietsch, *Levante-Handbuch* (Berlin, 1914), pp. 187-8. In 1914 there were over 1,700 German settlers in Palestine in agricultural colonies. They prospered so well as 'to excite the resentment of the natives.' (W. H. Dawson, *The Evolution of Modern Germany* (1911), p. 344.)
9. Alois Sprenger, *Babylonien, das reichste Land in der Vorzeit* (Heidelberg, 1886).
10. Carl Kaerger, *Kleinasien, ein deutsches Kolonisationsfeld* (Berlin, 1892).
11. Carl Kannenberg, *Kleinasiens Naturschätze* (Berlin, 1897).

12. *Deutschlands Ansprüche an das türkische Erbe* (Munich, 1896). Some English and French writers have considered this to be a document of importance, but an American historian of the Pan-German League considers that the pamphlet 'was not made much of even by the League and is of no particular importance.' (M. S. Wertheimer, *The Pan-German League* (New York, 1924), p. 170.)

13. Quoted by H. Feis, *Europe, The World's Banker 1870-1914* (New Haven: Yale University Press, 1930), p. 331.

14. It was not until 1913-14 that the German bondholders felt strong enough to demand that they should have a second representative on the Council of the Turkish Public Debt Administration and that a German should be President of the Council in rotation with the British and French representatives. Nothing came of the proposal.

15. The *Deutsche Bank* was also interested in the Bank for Oriental Railways (Zürich) which was used to finance the Anatolian Railway. The *Württembergische Vereinsbank* (Stuttgart) was associated with the *Deutsche Bank* in acquiring railway rights in the Balkans.

16. Memorandum by Sir Adrian Block to the British Government: see H. Feis, op. cit., pp. 321-2.

17. In the Russo-Turkish War (1877-8) the Turkish artillery was composed of 'Krupp's steel breech-loaders' which were 'superior to the bronze pieces of the Russians.' F. V. Greene, *The Campaign in Bulgaria 1877-8* (1903), p. 3.

18. A Turk told a French journalist: 'Mon grand-père a acheté sa sacoche à un Francais; il l'a payée deux livres; elle était en cuir. Mon père l'a achetée à un Anglais; il l'a payée une livre; elle était en toile cirée. Moi, je l'ai achetée à un Allemand; je l'ai payée deux medjidiés (huit francs); elle est en carton verni.' (Gaulis, *La Ruine d'un Empire*, p. 143, quoted by J. A. R. Marriott in *The Eastern Question* (1930), p. 395.)

19. This distinguished soldier and scholar crowned his career by defeating Townsend at Kut in 1916. He died at Baghdad shortly afterwards.

20. Marschall to von Hohenlohe, 5 March, 1898, in E. T. S. Dugdale, *German Diplomatic Documents 1871-1914* (1929), II, 467-8. For Marschall's work at Constantinople see E. Lindow, *Freiherr Marschall von Bieberstein als Botschafter in Konstantinopel 1897-1912* (Danzig, 1934).

21. The tour was arranged by Messrs. Thos. Cook and Co. Apparently in 1898 no German travel agency had developed its business in the Near East sufficiently to undertake the organization of such a tour.

22. It may be observed that the German scheme was a revival of an earlier British project. A Euphrates Valley Railway Company had been formed in 1854 to connect the Mediterranean and the Persian Gulf by rail (see Sir W. P. Andrew, *Memoir on the Euphrates Valley Railway Route* (1857), and articles in the *National Review*, XXXIX, 432-73; *Quarterly Review*, Oct. 1917, and the *United Empire*, July 1917, pp. 425-32). In 1872 a Parliamentary Committee reported favourably on a similar scheme. In 1879 a Euphrates Valley Association was formed.

23. A short section of the line (Scutari to Ismit) had been opened by the Turks in 1873. It was reported in 1913 that 'since the construction of the port of Haidar Pasha, Ismit has lost a great deal of its importance'. (*Report for 1913 on the Trade of the Consular District of Constantinople*, Cmd. 7048-191 of 1914.)

24. The Baghdad Railway Convention of 5 March, 1903 and the most important articles of the Statutes of the Imperial Ottoman Baghdad Railway Company are printed by Angus Hamilton, *Problems of the Middle East* (1909), pp. 452-80.

25. G. P. Gooch and Harold Temperley, *British Documents on the Origins of the War*, IV, p. 357.

26. Ibid. VI, p. 325.

27. The Germans were financially interested in this scheme: see Sir Thomas Holdich, *Boundaries in Europe and the Near East* (1918), p. 211.

28. Helfferich to von Gwinner, 30 November, 1908, in E. T. S. Dugdale, op. cit. III, p. 365.

29. See Alwyn Parker, 'The Bagdad Railway Negotiations' (*Quarterly Review*, October 1917) and documents in Gooch and Temperley, op. cit., x (pt. ii), pp. 329-402. The Anglo-German agreement of 1914 was initialled but owing to the outbreak of war it was never signed. Among the points settled in 1914 were the following: (*a*) two British subjects were to be appointed to the Board of the Baghdad Railway Company; (*b*) the line would not be continued beyond Basra without Great Britain's consent; (*c*) a company (with half its capital in British hands) would be formed by Lord Inchcape to control the Tigris-Euphrates navigation; and (*d*) the Turkish Petroleum Company (in which the Anglo-Persian Oil Company and a German-Dutch group would hold equal shares) would exploit Mesopotamia's petroleum resources (see E. M. Earle, 'The Turkish Petroleum Company' in the *Political Science Quarterly*, June 1924).

30. See Lovat Fraser, 'The Position in the Persian Gulf' (*National Review*, vol. I., 1907); 'Why help the Bagdad Railway?' (ibid., vol. LVII, 1911); and 'The Baron and his Bagdad Railway' (ibid., vol. LIX, 1912).

31. See Paul Rohrbach, *Der deutsche Gedanke in der Welt: Die Bagdadbahn* (Berlin, 1903; Leipzig, 1910); André Chéradame, *Le Chemin de fer de Bagdad* (Paris, 1903); A. Murabet, *Le Chemin de fer de Bagdad* (Brussels, 1913); C. A. Schaefer, *Die Entwicklung der Bagdadbahn Politik* (Weimar, 1916); Morris Jastrow, *The War and the Bagdad Railway* (Philadelphia, 1917); K. H. Müller, *Die wirtschaftliche Bedeutung der Bagdadbahn* (Hamburg, 1917); E. M. Earle, *Turkey, the Great Powers and the Bagdad Railway* (New York, 1923); Karl Helfferich, *Georg von Siemens* (3 vols.; Berlin, 1923); J. B. Wolf, *The Diplomatic History of the Bagdad Railway* (University of Missouri Studies, April 1936, XI (ii)); L. Ragey, *La question du chemin de fer de Bagdad 1893-1914* (Paris, 1936) and documents in G. P. Gooch and Harold Temperley, op. cit., II, 174-96.

32. Sir George Macmunn and Cyril Falls, *Military Operations. Egypt and Palestine* . . . (1928), I, 211. There is a chapter on the Hejaz Railway in Angus Hamilton, *Problems of the Middle East* (1909), pp. 273-92.

33. The little port of Haifa had at that time only an open roadstead but it had the advantage of being protected by the promontory of Mount Carmel.

34. *Report for 1913 on the Trade of the Consular District of Constantinople* (Cmd. 7048-191 of 1914), p. 26.

35. *Die Baumwolle in Klein-Asien* (reports of the *Deutsch-Levantinische Baumwollgesellschaft* to the Brussels Cotton Congress of 1910) and *Die Baumwollfrage* (*Veröffentlichungen des Reichskolonialamtes*, no. I; Jena, 1911).

36. Prince Bernhard von Bülow declared with typical enthusiasm in his book on *Imperial Germany* (English trans. 1914) that the Euphrates-Tigris region could 'hardly be surpassed for fertility and for its great possibilities of development in the future.' 'If one can speak of boundless possibilities anywhere, it is in Mesopotamia' (p. 96).

37. The *Deutsche Orientbank* of Berlin and Hamburg (linked with the *National-bank für Deu schland* of Berlin) had overseas branches in Constantinople, Dedeagatch, Aleppo, Minich, Tenteh, Beni-Souef, Mansourah, Brussa, Alexandria, Cairo, Tangier, Casablanca and Tehran.

38. Germany's trade with Turkey was of course only a tiny fraction of her total overseas trade. In 1910 Germany's imports from European Turkey represented 0·2 per cent. and her imports from Asiatic Turley 0·5 per cent of her total imports. In the same year Germany's exports to European Turkey were 1 per cent. and to Asiatic Turkey 0·4 per cent. of her total exports (Table in Werner Sombart, *Die deutsche Volkswirtschaft im 19en Jahrhundert* . . . (6th ed.; Berlin, 1923), pp. 526-7).

39. Erich Brandenburg, *From Bismarck to the World War* . . . *1870-1914* (1927), p. 457. Adana, however, is not a seaport.

40. For the struggle for spheres of influence in Persia at this time see W. Morgan Shuster, *The Strangling of Persia* (1912).

41. Sir W. E. Goschen to Sir C. Harding, 14 April, 1910 in G. P. Gooch and Harold Temperley, op, cit., VI, 464.

42. See R. Machray, 'The Germans in Persia' (*Fortnightly Review*, 1916, pp. 342-53); G. Demorgny, *La Question Persane et la Guerre* (Paris, 1916); Christopher Sykes, *Wassmuss. The German Lawrence* (Tauchnitz ed. 1937) and B. G. Martin, *German-Persian Diplomatic Relations, 1873-1912* (1959). For Germany's trade with the Middle East see Table 10 in Appendix.

Chapter VII

THE WAR ECONOMY OF GERMAN EAST AFRICA, 1914-1917

THE economic development of tropical African territories in the early days of their exploitation by white men was fostered by European and American capital. These colonies imported the manufactured goods that they needed and exported tropical raw materials and foodstuffs. It might be supposed that an African territory cut off from the outside world could not long survive. East Africa was in this position between the outbreak of the first World War and the expulsion of the German troops by the Allies in November 1917. The way in which the colony maintained its civil administration and supported an efficient military force in the field in these years is not without interest.

German East Africa was 384,000 square miles in area. The coastal districts and the valleys running into the Indian Ocean were hot, moist, unhealthy forest regions.[1] Beyond the hills running close to the 500 miles of East Africa's coast were plains with savannah vegetation in the north-east and less fertile country in the south and west. In the far west forest-covered hills had to be crossed before the rift valley (in which lay Lake Tanganyika) was reached.

The native population was about 7,500,000 in 1914. In the south lived Bantu tribes who were arable farmers. In the north the most important tribes were light-coloured Hamites (Masai, Galeas, Somalis) who raised cattle. On the coast were the Swaheli (of Semetic origin) whose language was the *lingua franca* of East Africa. Only about 170,000 natives were employed by Europeans or Indians.[2]

The native population was unevenly distributed. In Tanganyika five-sixths of the natives lived in the one-fifth of the country possessing satisfactory domestic water. Two-thirds of the territory, with poor domestic water, supported only eighteen per cent. of the total population. About 214,000 square miles, mainly large continuous blocks in the centre and west, were virtually unfit for human settlement.[3]

In 1913 most of the 5,336 white inhabitants[4] lived in the Dar-es-Salaam district (1,053) and in the highlands served by the Usambara Railway (1,971).[5] The coloured non-native population was 14,898, including 8,784 Indians, most of whom were petty traders living on the coast.[6]

East Africa had an adverse trade balance in 1913, imports being valued at £2,667,950 and exports at £1,777,500. The chief exports were sisal-hemp (£535,600), rubber (£328,400), hides (£247,500), cotton, copra, coffee and groundnuts. Germany absorbed over half the exports (£1,046,050). The chief imports for native consumption were cotton cloth and garments (£759,400) and rice (£185,750). Materials for the construction of public works,[7] various machines for railways, plantations and factories were valued at £492,400. Imports consumed by white people were, except for tobacco products,[8] of little significance from the point of view of trade statistics. But imported medicines, tobacco and various foods[9] and drinks provided Europeans with some of the necessities and many of the amenities of life. Commerce was mainly concentrated on the coast. Dar-es-Salaam served the area tapped by the Central Railway, which reached Kigoma on Lake Tanganyika in 1914. Tanga was the terminus of the railway to New Moshi, which served Usambara province.

In August 1914 East Africa was cut off from Germany by the British blockade.[10] The *Krönberg* (formerly *Rubens*) and the *Marie* were the only vessels that reached the colony. The former was attacked by British cruisers north of Tanga in April 1915. The ship sank in shallow water. Some of the cargo was lost but the rifles and ammunition were salvaged. In March 1916 medical and military supplies in the *Marie* reached Sudi Bay in the south of the colony. An attempt to send supplies from Germany by zeppelin failed.

The Germans in East Africa hoped to maintain some contact with the outside world through Mozambique, for Portugal was neutral until March 1916. Coastal trade stopped owing to the British blockade, and little success attended German efforts to use an overland route. Only one consignment of medical supplies reached German East Africa through Mozambique.[11]

The German forces in East Africa were 2,500 native troops (*askari*) under 260 German commissioned and non-commissioned officers, 2,000 native police and 3,500 Europeans who were called to the colours. The authorities had to provide from the resources of the territory food, clothing, medical supplies and ammunition to the troops and also secure supplies for the civilian (white and native) population. Fortunately for the Germans, unusually large supplies of various kinds had just been sent to Dar-es-Salaam in readiness for an exhibition to celebrate the completion of the Central Railway.

But when imported stocks had been consumed new supplies had to be produced locally.

The co-operation of the natives was essential. It was doubtful whether this could be secured, particularly in the south where there had been a serious rebellion a few years before. Experienced German officials feared that there would be native risings in the event of war with Britain, an opinion held also by Mr. King (British Consul at Zanzibar), who was well acquainted with conditions in German East Africa. But, apart from a few minor disturbances, the natives remained faithful to the Germans so long as they controlled East Africa.

When war broke out the Governor circularized every province to ascertain what food surpluses would be available for the troops and the European civilians. Local officials were instructed to foster native production of food. The replies to the inquiry showed that, except in Lindi province, where famine threatened owing to insufficient rainfall in the 1913-14 rainy season,[12] there were adequate surpluses of food which could be diverted from normal trade channels to meet the needs of the forces. It was unnecessary to ration native food supplies or to requisition food for the troops in the early days of the war. Depots were set up to buy food from the natives and in 1914-15 sufficient was obtained in this way. One difficulty was that at points served by the Central Railway (to which most of the food was brought) there were not enough mills to grind the native corn. So the grinding was done by hand by native women. European plantations supplied some maize. In 1914-15 in the region served by the Central Railway one-tenth of the food supplies came from plantations. Many cattle were bought in Ugogo, Kondoa-Irangi, Tabora and Muansa for the use of the troops.

The transport of food, fodder, medicines, arms and munitions to the front presented serious problems. Had the colony been invaded from the sea the Germans could have made full use of the Central and Usambara Railways. But after the failure of the Anglo-Indian expedition to Tanga (November 1914) the main Allied threat came by land from British East Africa (Kenya). To keep von Lettow Vorbeck's troops on the Kilimanjaro (northern) front adequately supplied Major-General Wahle, superintendent of the lines of communication, had to overcome two main difficulties. First, no railway joined the Central and Usambara lines. Secondly, coastal shipping between Dar-es-Salaam and Tanga ceased owing to the blockade. Supplies, therefore, had to go overland to the Kilimanjaro region. Transport by motor and oxen-wagon was very limited[13] and most supplies were carried by native porters. The principal routes used were those starting from Tabora, Dodoma and Morogoro, all on the Central Railway. The Tabora route ran to Muansa (Victoria Nyanza): the road from Dodoma ran through Kondoa Irangi and Arusha to New Moshi (inland terminus of the Usambara Railway): the Morogoro road led to Mombo and Korogwe. On the route to Korogwe at least 8,000 native porters were continuously employed. At first they took twelve days to transport loads from the Central Railway to the Usambara Railway. Later Lieutenant Kröber requisitioned light railway materials from large plantations, and a narrow gauge trolley line was constructed between Handeni and Mombo. Supplies now reached the Kilimanjaro front in nine days. The construction of the trolley line was also a useful preparation for eventual withdrawal from the northern front to the centre of the colony.

Throughout the first sixteen months of the war the military supply arrangements worked reasonably smoothly. But in 1915 the harvest in the north failed and early in February 1916 the troops on the Kilimanjaro front were faced with a shortage of food unless the usual additional supplies from the Central Railway could be rapidly increased. This involved the hasty recruitment of 20,000 more native carriers. About 2,000 of them died through being inadequately supplied with blankets. The military supply crisis was, however, overcome and this was fortunate for von Lettow Vorbeck, since it was in March 1916 that General Smuts launched his great offensive on the Kilimanjaro front.

The provision of foodstuffs for the European civilians also presented difficulties. Normally wheat, rye and rice were imported from Europe and India. Many of the whites on the coast used imported tinned milk, butter, vegetables and fruit. In August 1914 the colony was well provided with tinned foods since two large steamers had just arrived with extra supplies for the Dar-es-Salaam exhibition. The Governor and his colleagues were agreeably surprised at the extent to which local resources could supply the needs of the white inhabitants after existing imported stocks had been exhausted. The main problem was one of transport. Most of the Europeans lived in the Dar-es-Salaam region and in the Usambara highlands, and both these districts lay on the periphery of the colony. In the districts served by the Usambara Railway the production of foodstuffs increased. Coffee, wheat, fruit and potatoes were grown on plantations. Dairy produce came from the farms. Sausages and cooked meats were turned out in large quantities from factories in Wilhelmstal. But this extra produce was insufficient to feed the troops as well as the white civilians, and food had to be brought for consider-able distances to them.

Rice was grown in Muansa and Mahenge. Wheat and rye came from native farms in the remote highlands between Lakes Tangan-yika and Nyasa. Brown sugar was produced in the valleys of the Pangani, Rufiji and Lukuledi as well as in Muansa Province. Sugar refineries were established in the Pangani and Rufiji districts, the former under the guidance of a scientist from the Amani Agricul-tural Research Institute. Honey from wild bees was gathered by natives and this was a useful substitute for sugar. Milk and butter were also produced by the natives except in districts infested by the tsetse fly. Morogoro, which was an important civil and military administrative centre, was so short of dairy produce that white women and children were evacuated. Adequate supplies of locally produced fats and vegetable oils were available. Coffee came from European plantations in Usambara and salt from the Gottorp mines on the Central Railway. There was a shortage of vegetables owing to lack of seeds.

The problem of maintaining adequate supplies of medicines in the colony presented serious difficulties. Since malaria was wide-spread it was essential to have sufficient quinine available. Some cinchona had been planted in the gardens of the Amani Agricultural Research Institute, but it had been used only for experimental pur-poses and normally the colony imported quinine from Java. In 1915 quinine was being made at Mpapua by Dr. Schulze (the Government chemist) and at Amani by Dr. Marx (the chemist of the Institute). The Germans used about 1,000 kilogram of quinine in East Africa during the war. Half consisted of existing supplies and two consign-ments received by way of Mozambique and from the blockade runner *Marie*: half was produced locally.

It was only in the second half of 1915 that there was a shortage of cloth, garments, bandages and blankets. The construction of spinning wheels and handlooms was undertaken, much of the work being done by the Berlin Mission at Dar-es-Salaam. Government factories for spinning and weaving by hand were set up, the largest being at Morogoro and at the Miombo Cotton Institute (near Kilossa). Native children undertook the spinning and Indians were responsible for the weaving. The Miombo factory was producing 2,000 metres of cotton cloth a month before the Allied advance forced the Germans to give it up in the middle of 1916. In this way something was done to meet the cloth shortage. It was not found possible to manufacture blankets locally, and many native porters suffered during the rainy season from lack of adequate protection against the cold nights. Dyestuffs were made from native barks and from the roots of the *ndaa* tree. When existing supplies of khaki shirts were exhausted the military authorities arranged for large numbers of white shirts to be dyed brown. Footwear was manufactured on handicraft lines from cowhide, the tanning materials being secured from the mangroves in the coastal regions.

Many others articles normally imported by German East Africa were soon in short supply and considerable ingenuity was shown by the Germans in making substitutes locally from limited materials. The production of *ersatz* goods was by no means a monopoly of the Reich in the war of 1914. Petrol supplies, for example, soon came to an end. A planter named Schönheit invented a substitute (*trebol*) that was made from copra, but before it could be produced in any quantity his factory at Morogoro (erected with a government subsidy) fell into Allied hands. The shortage of tallow greatly reduced the production of candles. Beeswax, coconut oil and palm oil were used as substitutes. Soap, too, was made from materials produced in the colony. When no more imported jute sacks were available sacks were manufactured from bark. Sufficient tobacco was grown in East Africa to manufacture enough cigarettes for the white population so long as the whole colony was in German hands. Except for the products of Schultz's brewery at Dar-es-Salaam, most of the alcoholic drinks consumed in the colony were normally imported. In 1914-15 a number of small distilleries sprang up which manufactured various spirits from local materials such as palm wine and native grains.

The Amani Agricultural Research Institute did invaluable work in making products (and substitutes for products) normally imported. In the first eighteen months of the war the Institute 'prepared for use from its own products 16 varieties of foodstuffs and liquors, 11 varieties of spices, 12 varieties of medicines and medicaments, 5 varieties of rubber products, 2 of soap, oils and candles, 3 of materials used in making boots, and 10 miscellaneous substances. Many of these were prepared in comparatively large quantities, e.g. 15,200 bottles of "whiskey" (*sic*) and other alcoholic liquors, 10,252 lb. of chocolate and cocoa, 2,652 parcels of toothpowder, 10,000 pieces of soap, 300 bottles of castor oil, etc.'[14]

The war soon restricted commerce in German East Africa. Foreign trade stopped. Manufactured goods and tinned foods from Europe and cotton cloth and rice from India ceased to arrive. No sisal-hemp or other tropical products could be exported. Many firms closed down after selling existing stocks. But the Dar-es-Salaam house of Devers manufactured from native raw materials some products, such as sugar, which was normally imported. The cost of living rose and the Governor fixed the prices of tinned foods and cloth at 25 per cent. above those prevailing at the outbreak of war. But as supplies became very short black market activities increased. Planters who normally produced for the export market were soon in financial difficulties unless they could supply army needs. As Germans were called to the forces it became difficult to secure white supervisors, and some of the smaller plantations closed down. The shortage of civilian transport facilities, owing to the prior needs of the army, added to planters' difficulties. The German East Africa Company, however, maintained a limited number of its own plantations and also gave credit to some of the smaller planters.

The colonial administration did not have to raise money to pay for the campaign. That was the Reich's responsibility. Two main problems had to be faced locally. First, the administration was soon short of ready money, since the local revenue was reduced owing to the disappearance of income from import duties.[15] The German East Africa Bank of Dar-es-Salaam, however, gave the administration the necessary credit. Secondly, there was a shortage of banknotes, silver coins and small change, all of which were normally manufactured in Germany. When banknotes were worn out new ones were printed locally. To meet the shortage of silver coins small notes of various denominations were printed. But many natives would not accept notes. It was no easy matter to mint new coins in East Africa, but eventually the technical difficulties were overcome and a number of brass coins were produced.[16] Over 16,000 gold coins (15-rupee pieces) were also made. These 'Tabora sovereigns' were much sought after by the English after the conquest of the colony.[17]

Between August 1914 and March 1916 the whole of the colony remained in German hands. Then came the great Allied offensive. By September 1916 the Germans had lost six-sevenths of the territory and nine-tenths of the population of the colony. Only a corner in the south, the provinces of Kilwa, Lindi, Rufiji and Mahenge, remained in German hands and in the next twelve months this area gradually shrank until in November 1917 von Lettow Vorbeck's troops entered Portuguese territory. Non-combatants and most of the wounded soldiers were left in Allied hands, and when the colony was evacuated the fighting force was reduced to 278 Europeans, between 16,000 and 17,000 *askari* and about 4,000 porters. It had been no easy task to maintain the German troops in the field in the last stage of the campaign in German East Africa itself. The Germans relied for food upon the natives in the south of the colony, for European plantations were lacking in this region. There was a good harvest in 1916-17 and the efforts of the authorities to encourage the production of native foodstuffs achieved a considerable measure of success. Natives were sometimes not paid in cash for products commandeered by the troops.[18] But both white and native troops suffered hardships and were frequently on short rations. Wild game was hunted to provide occasional supplies of meat. Salt was obtained from sea water after the loss of the Gottorp mines. Vegetable oil was extracted from groundnuts. Hippopotamus and elephant fats were sometimes available. There was a shortage of many medicines, particularly quinine. Dr. Schultze produced from native materials several medicines and also toothpaste and shaving soap. Medical bandages were made at the Mahiwa Cotton Institute. Sacks and baskets were made from bark and grass. As far as transport was concerned many natives in the southern provinces were pressed into service as porters.

Thus for eighteen months the whole of the colony held out (and supported an efficient fighting force), although cut off from the outside world. For a rather longer period a small part of the territory maintained von Lettow Vorbeck's troops in the field. The Germans had every reason to be satisfied with the way in which the economic life of the colony was adapted to war conditions under most unfavourable circumstances. The efficiency of the civilian administration; the ingenuity of scientists, technicians and officials; the loyalty of the natives all contributed to secure this result.

REFERENCES

1. Sir Sydney Armitage-Smith remarked that Tanganyika Territory (ex-German East Africa without Ruanda-Urundi and Kionga) 'cannot conceivably be regarded as otherwise than unhealthy, and there are few officials who escape malaria . . .' (*Report . . . on a Financial Mission to Tanganyika . . .*, 26 September, 1932, Cmd. 4182 of 1932, p. 80).

2. 'From 13,000 to 16,000 were engaged in railway construction; about 3,000 were in mining; 5,000 were under government employment; 6,000 served in the police and military establishments; about 10,000 were in the employ of European merchants and missions; about 15,000 were carriers for native merchants; about 9,000 were domestic servants and about 10,000 more were employed by native, Arab and Indian traders' (R. L. Buell, *The Native Problem in Africa* (2 vols., New York, 1928), I, p. 496).

3. C. Gillman, 'A population map of Tanganyika Territory' (in *Report of H.M. Government . . . to the Council of the League of Nations on the Administration of Tanganyika Territory for 1935* (Colonial No. 113 of 1936); Appendix IX, pp. 197-215.

4. The 5,336 whites included 4,107 Germans. The adult males included 733 civil and military officials, 498 missionaries and clergymen, 882 planters and settlers, 352 technicians, 355 artisans and 523 traders.

5. Arusha 500, Moshi 467, Tanga 581, Wilhelmstal 423 (total 1,971).

6. *Deutsches Kolonial-Lexikon*, I, 386-7.

7. i.e. iron and railway lines (£394,700) and cement (£54,000).

8. £43,850 in 1913.

9. e.g. flour, rice, sugar, tinned vegetables and fruit.

10. The British blockade of the East African coast was not formally proclaimed until February 1915.

11. Dr. Schnee (Governor of German East Africa) complained in his war memoirs (*Deutschostafrika im Weltkrieg*, p. 162) that 'the real ruler of Portuguese East Africa was Mr. MacDonnell, the English Consul-General, beside whom the continually changing Portuguese Governors were of only secondary importance.'

12. Arrangements were made to send food to Lindi province, but the scheme was only partially carried out since, when war broke out, the British blockade greatly restricted coastal shipping. It was not found possible to transport goods to the south by land. The 1914-15 rains were also inadequate and it was estimated that some 2,000 natives died of hunger in Lindi province.

13. The prevalence in the colony of the tsetse fly (carrier of the disease 'nagana' which was fatal to horses, mules and cattle) forced the Germans to transport supplies by rail and by native porters. But in the immediate vicinity of the Kilimanjaro front motor and oxen-wagon traffic was sufficiently heavy to warrant the construction from local materials of some new permanent bridges. Thus a stone and concrete arched bridge was built by the engineer Rentell over the Kikafu torrent (west of New Moshi).

14. *Report of the East Africa Commission*, Cmd. 2387 of 1925, p. 86.

15. On the other hand, the native hut and head taxes were collected throughout the territory in 1914 and 1915. A record revenue was secured from these sources in 1915.

16. Francis Brett Young (*Marching on Tanga* (new edition, 1940), p. 132) states that when General Smuts's troops broke through on the Kilimanjaro front in the spring of 1916 they came across 'the new German paper currency, notes of 5 rupees printed on rough greenish paper, also their *heller* pieces made from used Mauser cartridges'.

17. H. Schnee, op. cit., pp. 289-91; see also F. Wehling, *Entwicklung der Deutsch-Ostafrikanischen Rupie* (Münster, 1929) *passim*.

18. A German mission visited Tanganyika in 1925 to pay the *askari* arrears of pay, but it had no authority to meet claims concerning property requisitioned by German troops during the campaign (Sir Donald Cameron, *My Tanganyika Service . . .* (1938), pp. 66-8).

Chapter VIII

THE CONQUEST OF THE GERMAN COLONIES, 1914-18[1]

IN the first World War the colonial campaigns were dismissed as 'side-shows', while it was the Western Front in France and Belgium that claimed popular attention. The historians of the war of 1914 have on the whole neglected the operations in Africa and the Pacific which resulted in the Allied conquest of the German colonies. These campaigns are relegated to a footnote in Cruttwell's standard *History of the Great War* (1934). Only the operations in West Africa and the first part of the campaign in East Africa are fully described in the British official history of the war of 1914. Yet the conquest of the German colonial empire was accomplished by operations which called forth the highest military and personal qualities of the British and Allied forces, for they were conducted against a determined and resourceful enemy in face of great climatic and other natural difficulties.

The defence of the colonies against attack from Britain and her allies presented Germany with a serious problem in 1914. The white and native military and police forces in the overseas possessions were small, and their main function was to preserve internal order. In Africa the four German colonies were defended by only 11,000 German and native soldiers and policemen. These forces, scattered over a continent, were incapable of serious aggressive action against neighbouring colonies. Kiao Chow—with its naval base of Tsingtau—was the only powerfully armed German overseas possession. It was impossible to send reinforcements from Germany itself to the colonies so long as the British Navy commanded the seas. Germany hoped to gain a swift victory on the Western Front, and so not merely preserve, but even extend her overseas possessions.

The official view in Germany appears to have been that her weakness in Africa and the Pacific made it impossible to offer serious resistance to a determined attack. So an attempt was made to keep the colonies outside the range of hostilities. The German Government invoked Article 11 of the Berlin Congo Act of 1885, which provided that territories in the conventional Congo Basin should,

96

if possible, be 'under the rule of neutrality' in war-time. But no sanction had been provided to enforce this Article, and the signatories of the General Act had only agreed to use their good offices to prevent the spreading of hostilities to the Congo region. The Allies rejected German suggestions that no hostilities should take place in Africa. The German Government then told local commanders in the colonies to hold out as long as possible. Some enterprising colonial officials and soldiers hoped that Germany's overseas possessions might play a more ambitious role in time of war. They considered that the small colonial armies should attack enemy possessions, and so force the Allies to maintain in those regions troops which might otherwise have been used on the Western Front. Opportunities of assisting disaffected elements in neighbouring Allied territories should not be neglected. The local commanders in East and South West Africa—when left to their own devices after communications with Germany had been severed—worked on these lines, and they succeeded in inflicting much damage upon the Allies. This was done despite certain pronounced differences between local civil and military authorities in the German colonies. Thus in East Africa the supreme military power was in the hands of the civilian Governor (Dr. Schnee), who did not work smoothly with the military commander (General von Lettow Vorbeck). In the Cameroons the military authorities appear to have held the civilian administrators in contempt.

Since the Allies were eventually able to overrun the whole of the German colonial empire, there might have been grounds for imagining that Britain had planned some such action before the outbreak of war. Britain's command of the seas and the likelihood of disaffected native tribes assisting an invader were factors favouring such an enterprise. In fact, no general plan for the conquest of Germany's overseas possessions existed in 1914. Immediately war was declared, however, the Offensive Sub-Committee of the Committee of Imperial Defence was set up to recommend to the Cabinet plans for joint military and naval operations in enemy territory. The Committee advised first that only troops available in neighbouring British possessions should be used for offensive operations against German colonies and, secondly, that the object of such operations should be to deprive Germany of the use of important coaling and telegraph stations, so as to hamper the activities of German cruisers and commerce-raiders on the high seas. When this was accomplished more ambitious schemes of colonial conquest were undertaken.

Before the German colonial empire and German influence overseas could be destroyed it was necessary to round up those units of
the enemy fleet which were at large on the high seas at the outbreak
of war. The German China Squadron (commanded by Admiral
Graf von Spee) was at the Caroline Islands in August 1914. Owing
to Japan's entry into the war on the Allied side, this squadron could
not use its main base at Tsingtau. Von Spee molested neither the
Australian expedition against New Guinea nor the New Zealand
expedition against Samoa. He went to the west coast of South
America, where he defeated Admiral Craddock's weaker squadron
off Coronel, only to be himself destroyed by Admiral Sturdee off
the Falkland Islands. Thus the danger of German naval intervention against Allied expeditions to the German colonies was removed.

Meanwhile the first moves against Germany's overseas possessions
were being made. Togoland, the smallest of the German colonies
in Africa, fell to the Allies after a brief campaign.[2] The Germans
had at their disposal an armed native constabulary of some 500 men,
and most of the 300 German residents in the colony had had some
military training. Britain was in a position to bring a much larger
force than this into the field from the Gold Coast and Nigeria. The
Gold Coast Regiment (West African Frontier Force) alone included
50 British officers and men and 2,000 native ranks and reservists.
The original British plan of operations—designed to stop the Germans from invading the Gold Coast and cutting our communications
on the lower Volta—contemplated the seizure of Lome and the
isolation of Northern Togoland. But this plan had been drawn up
before the completion of the powerful wireless station at Kamina,
which, as the Governor of the Gold Coast Colony observed, was
'destined to be the pivotal point of the German world-wide wireless
system.' When war broke out the Offensive Sub-Committee of the
Committee of Imperial Defence at once recommended that our
Gold Coast forces should attack Togoland with the main object of
destroying the Kamina wireless station.

The Germans gave up Lome and the coast without fighting, and
retired 75 miles inland to Khra village to defend Kamina. They
were followed by a British force of 650 men (under Lieutenant-
Colonel Bryant) and a French force of 370 men (under Major
Maroix). The British advanced along the Lome-Atakpame railway
and suffered 75 casualties when the Germans counter-attacked at
Khra village. But this was the only action of any importance. The
allied forces converged upon Kamina, which was surrendered by

Major von Doering on 26 August, 1914, after the wireless station had been completely destroyed.

It might have been expected that the Germans would have offered a much more serious resistance in Togoland. Major von Doering was well acquainted with the difficult jungle in which the operations were conducted. Although the native tribes of the interior showed comparatively little enthusiasm for the German cause, the native soldiers, police and other employees were, on the whole, faithful. On the other hand, the Germans were unfortunate in losing Captain Pfaeler—who was really conducting the operations—in an early engagement. Their intelligence service broke down, and they could not induce natives to go to the Gold Coast for information. Consequently they over-estimated the size of the Allied forces opposing them. The rapid conquest of Togoland was no hopeful augury for the future of the German colonies.

The Cameroons[3] was a far harder nut for the Allies to crack than Togoland. The conquest of a tropical African colony half as big again as Germany itself presented many difficulties. Geographical conditions favoured the Germans. The swamps and jungles of the coastal region and the great mountain range on the Nigerian frontier were obstacles to invasion both by sea and by land. The neutral territory of Rio Muni (Spanish Guinea)—an enclave in the German colony—was a useful base for supplies and news. Until the Allied blockade was tightened up, the Spanish island of Fernando Po also proved to be a valuable link with the outside world. The principal tribes in the interior of the Old Cameroons were loyal to the Germans. The military force at the disposal of the Germans included 200 white and 1,650 native troops, as well as 30 German and 15 native armed police.

In view of the difficulties involved, the Offensive Sub-Committee of the Committee of Imperial Defence decided that our first objectives should be Duala, Victoria, and Buea. These three towns and the neighbouring plantations were the political and commercial heart of the Cameroons. Their seizure would cripple the German administration of the colony—with the possible exception of the South—and would be a first step to further conquests. In the region first selected for attack the Allies could hope, with some confidence, for support from the sorely oppressed Duala tribe, which had never settled down under German rule. Rudolf Bell, the leader of the tribe, was executed for high treason by the Germans at the outbreak of war.

An Anglo-French expeditionary force under General Dobell

seized Duala at the end of September 1914 after the British light cruiser *Challenger* had successfully negotiated both the natural obstacles and the wreck-barrage in the Cameroons estuary. The German military Commander (Major Zimmermann) and the Governor (Ebermaier) left for the interior with most of the German troops, armaments, stores and provisions. After this initial success the Allies decided to attempt the conquest of the whole of the colony. By the end of 1914 they had seized the Mount Cameroon plantation region (including Buea, the seat of the administration) as well as the Northern Railway to Nkogsamba and the Central Railway to Edea. These achievements cost the Allies only 41 white and 389 native troops.

Although the Allies had gained important successes, it must be remembered that their scattered columns were operating in very difficult country. It was not easy for them to co-operate satisfactorily. The smaller German forces, well armed with machine-guns, were working on interior lines, and were still in contact with Rio Muni. In the spring of 1915 an attempt was made to secure closer co-operation between the Allied forces operating in different parts of the Cameroons. It was arranged that joint action should be taken against Garua (a strongly fortified post in the North) and Jaunde (the new seat of the administration in the South). Garua was surrendered by von Crailsheim in June 1915, but the advance against Jaunde failed, the Allies suffering some 900 casualties.

There was a lull in the operations during the rainy season (July-September) of 1915. General Dobell gave some of his native troops leave to their homes in Nigeria and the Gold Coast. Some of those who remained were able to enjoy a period of rest. Others co-operated with the navy in tightening the blockade of the Cameroons. The Germans used the respite given by the rains to make careful preparations to defend Jaunde to the last. By October 1915 arrangements had been made to renew the Allied attack. General Dobell's main force, based on Duala, operated in three columns under Colonel Gorges, Colonel Mayer, and Lieutenant-Colonel Cotton. At the same time General Aymérich's French and Belgian forces resumed their advance from Gaboon and the Middle Congo. The Allies succeeded in occupying Jaunde on new year's day of 1916, but they failed to capture the German troops. Zimmermann made a brilliant withdrawal to the neutral territory of Rio Muni, 130 miles away. No fewer than 975 Germans (including 400 non-combatants) and 14,000 native soldiers and carriers succeeded in this way in avoiding capture. In February 1916 Captain von Raben surrendered the fortress of Mora, and so fell the last German stronghold in the Cameroons.

In eighteen months Allied military and naval forces had cleared the enemy out of a colony 305,000 square miles in extent. Relying upon forces raised in neighbouring territories, and operating in difficult country, they had overcome strong German resistance. The Germans, cut off from their homeland, had made the most vigorous efforts to keep an army in the field as long as possible, so that in the event of an early peace they might claim the retention of the colony. Many of the natives saw the Germans ejected without regret, but the Jaunde, in whose territory the Germans made their last stand, remained faithful to the end. Ebermaier and Zimmermann had kept considerable Allied forces employed for a year and a half, and had defended the Cameroons with energy and determination.[4]

Meanwhile the South West African campaign[5] had also been brought to a successful conclusion. Great Britain and the Union of South Africa both considered that it was essential to attack this territory. Britain desired the speedy destruction of the colony's wireless stations—e.g., the powerful transmitter at Windhoek—which might give information to commerce-raiders in the Atlantic. South Africa feared Germany's ambitions in Central and Southern Africa. She wished to end German rule in South West Africa, and so remove a threat to her own safety. By a strange twist of fortune, the mantle of Cecil Rhodes had fallen upon Smuts and Botha—the two Boer generals who had only recently fought to maintain the independence of their people against the rising tide of British Imperialism.

The main difficulty of conducting a campaign in South West Africa was to secure the transport, over long distances, of supplies of food and water to troops operating in desert regions. While the Germans could threaten the Union only across the land frontier, the British could attack by land and sea. Both sides hoped to obtain help from malcontents living within the enemy's frontiers. The Germans hoped to enlist the aid of discontented Boers, whose grievances they had long been secretly exploiting.[6] The South Africans expected co-operation from the sorely oppressed natives of South West Africa, whose grievances were so serious that the Germans lived in continual fear of rebellion. In fact during the war there was a Boer rising against the Union Government, and the Bastards of Rehoboth revolted against their German masters.

The combatants were unevenly matched in military resources. Conscription had been introduced in South Africa in 1912. During

101

the war 6,533 officers, 69,834 white men, and 33,546 coloured troops were sent on service to South West Africa. These forces were far superior to those at the disposal of the Germans. During the Herero revolt there had been as many as 15,000 German troops in the colony, but by 1914 the local Defence Force had been reduced to some 2,000 men. There was also a Police Force of 300 men. On the outbreak of war about 3,000 German settlers were incorporated in the Defence Force. Germany could hardly contemplate serious aggression against the Union of South Africa with a force of 5,000 or 6,000 men. Any colonial territorial gains which Germany might secure after a victorious war would clearly result from German successes on the Continent, and not from military action against South Africa. Dr. Seitz, the Governor of South West Africa, was, however, determined that the colony should not fall an easy prey to the Union of South Africa. His object was to keep South African troops occupied as long as possible, so that they might not be available in a more important theatre of war. This result might be attained by raids on South African territory, by helping Boer malcontents in the Union, and by resisting invasion to the last.[7]

On the outbreak of war the South African Government planned a threefold attack upon South West Africa. This failed. It is true that a Union expedition (which came by sea from Cape Town) captured Lüderitz Bay, and subsequently reinforcements—led by the veteran Sir Duncan M'Kenzie—advanced cautiously from this town along the railway to Garub. On the other hand, the Germans captured Walfish Bay and successfully resisted two attempts of the South Africans to invade South West Africa across the Orange River. General Lukin seized Raman's Drift, only to be cut off and defeated at Sandfontein, while Lieutenant-Colonel Maritz (whose task was to take Schuit's Drift) turned traitor, proclaimed the independence of the Transvaal and the Orange Free State, and made an agreement with the Governor of South West Africa. The defection of Maritz and the Boer rebellion (under Beyers and De Wet) delayed the Union's projected invasion of South Africa.[8]

By the end of 1914 the Union Government, having put down the Boer rebellion, resumed its plans for attacking South West Africa from another point—the British port of Walfish Bay (which the Germans had occupied). An expeditionary force, under Colonel Skinner, successfully landed there on Christmas Day 1914. Swakopmund, 20 miles away, was captured on 13 January, 1915. The Germans now made a counter-attack upon the Union. They crossed the Orange River at Schuit's Drift and reached Upington, 100 miles within the Union territory. Here General Deventer defeated the Germans and their Boer allies. A German attack on Kakamas was also repulsed. Thus the Germans failed in their counter-offensive. Their forces and equipment were inadequate to enable them to take full advantage of the Union's difficulties in the early months of the war.

Early in February 1915 Botha was able to take over the active direction of operations, and the second phase of the campaign began. There could be no doubt as to the outcome of the struggle. The Germans had lost two of their senior officers—von Heydebreck and von Raphard—and were now led by Lieutenant-Colonel Franke. Their Boer allies had failed them, and their southern flank was exposed. They had now only some 4,000 troops available, and could expect little support from the native population. Indeed, the Bastards of Rehoboth revolted in April 1915.⁹ The Germans were cut off from their homeland, and their supplies of food and ammunition were limited. Botha commanded vastly superior forces. His problem was to secure his long lines of communication while operating in peculiarly difficult country and to bring to bay as quickly as possible the small but agile enemy forces.

The colony was attacked from both the south and the west. The southern advances from Upington and Garub had by April 1915 resulted in the capture of the chief missionary and trading-posts of Great Namaqualand. Only at Gibeon did the Germans put up a stiff resistance and inflicted heavy losses on the Union troops (26 April, 1915). On the same day Botha advanced from Swakopmund upon Windhoek, the capital of the colony, which he captured on 11 May. At the same time Skinner seized the Otavi Railway. The back of the German resistance had been broken, but a further operation was necessary to round up the German forces which had escaped to the northern part of the colony. After two months of careful preparation, Botha opened the last phase of the campaign on 18 June, 1915. His advance northward was made with remarkable rapidity. By 30 June, Otavi, the centre of the valuable copper-mines, had been captured, Botha now gave Franke the opportunity to capitulate, and he did so, a local armistice being signed. Shortly afterwards Myburgh seized Tsumeb and Brits occupied Namutoni. The British casualties in this campaign (and the suppression of the Boer rebellion) amounted to 137 officers and 1,632 other ranks. Of these, 62 officers and 498 other ranks were wounded. The cost of the campaign was about £15,000,000.

By the capitulation of Korab the Germans agreed to the surrender of their military stores and equipment. The German forces were demobilized, but kept their rifles.[10] German civilians were allowed to return to their homes. The survival of German settlements in South West Africa was thus assured. Some 6,350 Germans were deported during and immediately after the war, but they were for the most part soldiers, policemen, and officials. The census of 1921 showed that 7,000 Germans remained in South West Africa.

The conclusion of the campaign in South West Africa enabled the Union to devote more attention to the operations in East Africa.[11] Here the subjugation of the Germans proved to be a difficult task. The operations lasted throughout the war. In 1914 Germany's largest colony was defended by 2,500 coloured troops led by 260 German commissioned and non-commissioned officers. The Police Force numbered 2,000 natives. During the war some 3,000 German residents and visitors were called to the colours. The number of natives under arms was increased to about 12,000. The native soldiers (*askari*) employed by the Germans remained faithful to their masters throughout the arduous campaign. As in other colonies, so in East Africa the task of the local military forces was to maintain internal order. But von Lettow Vorbeck, the German Commander, recognized that it would be possible not only to defend East Africa, but also to take offensive action against neighbouring British colonies.

Various circumstances favoured such an enterprise. The British had no large military forces permanently established in East Africa. The East African Rifles numbered only some 3,000 officers and men, and they were distributed between British East Africa, Uganda, and Nyasaland. On the northern frontier a British offensive would have to overcome the natural obstacles of Mount Kilimanjaro and the Pare Hills. The Germans, on the other hand, could hope to cut the Uganda Railway (Mombasa-Kisumu), which ran temptingly close to the frontier. In the west the Germans were able, for a time, to command the waters of Lake Tanganyika. In the south lay the Portuguese territory of Mozambique, from which little was to be feared. The long Indian Ocean coastline gave opportunities for blockade-running.

Operations began at sea on 8 August, 1914, when two small British cruisers (the *Astræa* and *Pegasus*) bombarded Dar-es-Salaam, the capital of the colony. Meanwhile the small light German cruiser *Königsberg* (Captain Max Looff), which had left Dar-es-Salaam just before war broke out, was raiding shipping in the Indian Ocean. In September the *Königsberg* appeared off Zanzibar, destroyed the *Pegasus*, and then sought refuge in the Rufiji delta. There she was found by three powerful British cruisers in October. But it was not until July 1915 that the British, after repeated attacks with two monitors, succeeded in destroying the German cruiser. In this operation a seaplane was for the first time used to direct gunfire.[12] On land the first operations of importance were on the northern (Kilimanjaro) front, where the Germans outnumbered the British. Von Lettow Vorbeck seized Taveta, raided the Uganda Railway and threatened Mombasa. In November 1914 an Anglo-Indian expedition of some 8,000 men made an assault from the sea upon the port of Tanga, which was the terminus of the Usambara Railway and the best base for German operations against British East Africa. The Germans hastily sent reinforcements to Tanga. The invaders were ambushed, and were decisively defeated, with heavy losses of men and material. The British then prepared to attack Tanga by land, and concentrated troops south of Jassini, but the Germans dislodged them in January 1915.

Vast preparations were made in 1915 for the conquest of German East Africa. British, South African, Indian and native troops— well equipped with modern arms, munitions, vehicles and stores— were assembled in British East Africa for the main thrust from the north. The construction of a new branch line of the Uganda Railway from Voi towards Taveta was undertaken. Subsidiary attacks by the British from Northern Rhodesia and Nyasaland and by the Belgians from the Congo were planned. Over 70,000 troops and porters were brought together to crush the small forces at the disposal of von Lettow Vorbeck. General Smuts, the commander-in-chief, reached the scene of operations in British East Africa in February 1916. On his staff were Collyer, van Deventer, and Beyers, who had done excellent work in the South West African campaign.

The object of the Allied offensive was to seize the Central Railway (Dar-es-Salaam—Kigoma), and so cripple the German hold upon their East African colony. On the northern front, where the main assault was delivered, Smuts's first task was to seize New Moshi, the terminus of the railway to Tanga. The operations against New Moshi began on 8 March, 1916. The Latema-Reata Pass (the gap between Mount Kilimanjaro and the Pare Hills) was forced and the railhead was taken on 13 March. Then an attack was made along the Usambara Railway and the River Ruwu-Pangani, with the object of seizing the German defensive positions in the Pare and Usambara Hills, and so gaining control of the Usambara region, which contained rich coffee, banana, tobacco, rubber, and sisal-hemp plantations. This operation was successfully completed in July, 1916.

Meanwhile van Deventer's mounted division took Kondoa Irangi 29 April, 1916, while Smuts himself captured Handeni (19 June), on the route to Morogoro. Von Lettow Vorbeck tried to hold up Smuts's thrust towards the Central Railway by taking up a position in the forests of the Nguru Mountains. Smuts and Brits resumed the offensive early in August 1916, and tried to encircle von Lettow Vorbeck's troops at Kanga (in the Nguru Mountains), but the Germans slipped out of the net. Von Lettow Vorbeck retreated to Morogoro. Once more Smuts tried to encircle his elusive foe. The German line of retreat southwards lay along two main routes, one on each side of the Uluguru Mountains, and Smuts attempted to cut both routes. Again the pincers' movement to entrap the Germans failed, and von Lettow Vorbeck made good his retreat to the River Ruwu.[13] This position he held for the remainder of 1916. In the autumn the British seized all the important points on the East African coast—including Bagamojo, Dar-es-Salaam, Kilwa and Lindi—and the Belgians captured Tabora, so completing the Allied control of the Central Railway.

By his offensive of 1916 Smuts conquered 85 per cent. of the territory and 90 per cent. of the native population of German East Africa. The capital, the coastline, the Central and Usambara Railways, the Great Lakes and the districts from which the best porters were drawn were all in Allied hands. Only the south-eastern portion of the colony remained under German control. Allied casualties (both through fighting and sickness) had been heavy. Moreover, Smuts had failed to annihilate von Lettow Vorbeck's small forces. All his encircling movements had been frustrated. If Smuts imagined that the campaign was virtually over when he laid down his command in January 1917 he under-estimated the resourcefulness of von Lettow Vorbeck and the courage and tenacity of the troops he commanded.

In 1917 the Germans were cleared out of the last corner of the colony. They fought rearguard actions—for example, at Narüngombe and Mahiwa—with great skill, and more than once evaded encirclement.[14] But they were far too weak to prevent the steady advance of their enemies. At the end of November 1917 von Lettow Vorbeck abandoned the German colony and invaded Mozambique with the remnants of the main German force. This consisted of 278 Europeans, some 16,000 *askari*, about 4,000 porters, 1,000 women and boys.

The operations after November 1917 were of little military significance. The Allies held all German East Africa, and their hold on the colony could not be shaken. They made every effort to round up the remnant of the German troops still at large. For von Lettow Vorbeck it was a matter of prestige to avoid capture and to maintain a force in the field. By keeping up a struggle to which there could be only one ending, he made the Allies maintain much larger forces in East Africa than would otherwise have been necessary. For ten months the Germans operated in Mozambique, replenishing their stores and arms at the expense of the Portuguese. Von Lettow Vorbeck marched through almost the whole length of Mozambique from north to south. Then he returned to the upper Rovuma, marched through the south-west of German East Africa and finally invaded Northern Rhodesia. Here the news of the Armistice brought the campaign to a close.

So ended the greatest of the African 'side-shows'. The conquest of German East Africa is said to have cost the Allies £75,000,000. British casualties amounted to 967 officers and 17,650 other ranks, of whom 614 officers and 7,263 other ranks were wounded. In addition, over 40,000 native followers lost their lives. In comparison with the great battles on the Western Front, the East African campaign was of minor significance, but at any other time it would have been regarded as a major operation. The honours of the campaign were not unevenly divided. In a few months in 1916 Smuts conquered nearly the whole of a great colony, despite the opposition of an intrepid foe, the difficulties of transport, and the unhealthy climate. Von Lettow Vorbeck, on the other hand, brilliantly fulfilled the task which he had set himself. Cut off from Germany, and without hope of receiving reinforcements, he kept vastly superior numbers of the enemy occupied throughout the war. In his account of the struggle he claimed that the Allies had used against him 130 generals and 300,000 men. He had the satisfaction of maintaining an army in the field to the very end. Friend and foe recognized in him a master of bush warfare.

It has been seen that South African forces played an important part in the conquest of both South West and East Africa. In the same way the Dominions of Australia and New Zealand undertook the main responsibility for the seizure of Germany's scattered possessions in the Pacific Ocean.[15] As these colonies had wireless, cable, and coaling stations, it was in the interest of the Allies that they should be captured as quickly as possible. The German military forces in these territories were insignificant, and no resistance was to be expected from them. But so long as von Spee's squadron was at large, the sending of naval expeditions to seize Germany's colonies in the Pacific entailed certain risks. A small New Zealand expedition of 1,383 men, protected by the *Montcalm* (a French cruiser), *Australia* (the most powerful warship then in the Pacific), and *Melbourne*, took the Samoan islands of Opolu and Savaii at the end of August 1914 without meeting any opposition. A fortnight later the *Scharnhorst* and *Gneisenau* appeared off Samoa, but the *Australia* and *Melbourne* had already returned to Sydney to protect two transports of some 1,500 Australian troops on their voyage to New Guinea. The Germans defended Rabaul wireless station, but it was captured without difficulty. Meanwhile the Japanese rounded up the Germans in the Ladrone, Caroline, Pelew, and Marshall Islands.

Kiao Chow,[16] Germany's only foothold on the Asiatic mainland, was well defended. There were coastal batteries to enable the naval base of Tsingtau to reply to attack from the sea. But only two small warships of von Spee's squadron were at Tsingtau when war broke out. The old Austrian cruiser *Kaiserin Elisabeth* was also in the port. The defences against land operations were also powerful, but they had been devised to withstand trouble from the Chinese rather than an attack from Japan. Captain Mayer-Waldeck, the Governor of Kiao Chow, had some 4,000 men to defend the territory. A Japanese fleet with the co-operation of British naval units blockaded Tsingtau, and a large Japanese expeditionary force, under General Kamio, was fitted out to seize the territory. The bulk of the expedition, including a British contingent, landed at Laoshan Bay. General Kamio conducted the siege of Tsingtau in a scientific and methodical manner. The advanced German positions were evacuated at the end of September 1914. A month later the main defences—the three forts on Moltke Hill, Bismarck Hill, and Iltis Hill—were subjected to a terrific bombardment. On 7 November the Germans surrendered, after scuttling their warships and blowing up the port installations.

Two aspects of the conquest of the German colonies deserve mention. First, as far as Great Britain was concerned, it was predominantly an Imperial enterprise. It was troops from the Dominions, from India, and from the Crown Colonies that bore the brunt of the struggle. South Africa, Australia, and New Zealand considerably extended their spheres of interest and their outlook on world politics as a result of these campaigns. Secondly, the determined resistance put up by local German commanders—particularly by von Lettow Vorbeck—against heavy odds caught the imagination of the German public. Before 1914 there had been much apathy in Germany concerning colonial enterprise. After the overseas possessions had been lost the memory of their defence helped to keep alive the colonial idea in Germany.

THE CONQUEST OF THE GERMAN COLONIES, 1914-18

REFERENCES

1. Particulars of the Defence Forces in the German colonies are given in the article on 'Schutztruppen' in the *Deutsches Kolonial-Lexikon* (edited by Dr. Heinrich Schnee, 3 vols., 1920), III, pp. 321-4, and in *Dreissig Jahre Deutsche Kolonialpolitik* (edited by Paul Leutwein), pp. 38-43.

2. For the Togoland campaign, see *Correspondence relating to the Military Operations in Togoland* (Parliamentary Paper 1915, Cd. 7872); 'La Conquête du Togoland' (in *Renseignements Coloniales*, supplement to *L'Afrique Française*, May 1915, pp. 82-102); Sir Charles Lucas, *The Empire at War*, IV (1924), pp. 18-51; E. H. Gorges, *The Great War in West Africa* (1930), ch. 2; F. J. Moberly, *Military Operations. Togoland and the Cameroons, 1914-16* (History of the Great War based on Official Documents, 1931), ch. 1; C. H. O'Neil, ch. 2; and E. Dane, ch. 8.

3. For the Cameroons campaign, see E. Dane, ch. 9; Sir Charles Lucas, IV, pp. 62-120; E. H. Gorges, ch. 3 onwards; F. J. Moberly, ch. 2 onwards; F. Q. Champness ('Guns, Q.F.C.'), 'Doing her Bit—An Account of a Cruiser's Operations in the Cameroons' (in *Blackwood's Magazine*, December 1915); 'Notes on the Cameroons' by a Member of the West African Expeditionary Force (in the *Geographical Journal*, XLVIII, 1916); Henri Mailier, 'Le rôle des colonies françaises dans la campagne du Cameroun' (in *L'Afrique Française*, June 1916, pp. 209-15); C. S. Stooks, 'From a Diary in the Cameroons' (in the *Cornhill Magazine*, October 1919, pp. 380-90); M. Schwarte and others, *Der Grosse Krieg* (8 vols., 1921-5), vol. IV; General J. Aymérich, *La Conquête du Cameroun* . . . (Paris, 1933); M. L. J. E. Weithas, *La Conquête du Cameroun et du Togo* (1931); J. Ferrandi, *Conquête du Cameroun Nord, 1914-15*, and the official Belgian history, *Les Campagnes Coloniales Belges, 1914-18* (Brussels, 1927, etc.).

4. According to F. J. Moberly (p. 426) the Allied military casualties in the Cameroons campaign were: 50 Europeans and 867 Africans (British and 68 Europeans and 838 Africans (French). These figures exclude both naval casualties and casualties among native porters. Aymérich (p. 194) states that the French casualties were: Europeans 118 (41 killed and 77 wounded), Africans 1,584 (474 killed and 1,110 wounded)—total 1,702.

5. For the campaign in German South West Africa, see W. B. Worsfold, 'The Taking of German South West' (in the *United Empire*, VI, 1915, pp. 747-51); Sir Maitland Park, 'German South West African Campaign' (in the *Journal of the African Society*, XV, 1916, pp. 113-32); P. A. Bridel, 'Notes sur la campagne du sud-ouest Africain' (in the *Bibliothèque Universelle et Revue Suisse*, vol. 82, Lausanne, 1916); Dr. H. F. B. Walker, *A Doctor's Diary in Damaraland* (1917); H. Whittall, *With Botha and Smuts in Africa* (1917); Theodor Seitz, *Südafrika im Weltkreig* (1920), and *Der Zusammenbruch in Deutsch Südwestafrika* (1920); Hans von Oelhafen, *Der Feldzug in Südwest, 1914-15* (1923); R. Hennig, *Deutsch-Südwestafrika im Weltkrieg* (1920); E. Dane, chs. 2 and 3; and Sir Charles Lucas, IV, pp. 434-58 (by J. Saxon Mills). For an interesting comparison of the geographical background of the campaigns in German South West Africa and the war between Peru and Chile (1879-83), see G. M. Wrigley, pp. 48-50.

6. See the *Report of the Judicial Commission of Enquiry into the* . . . *Recent Rebellion in South Africa* (Cape Town, December 1916), p. 82 and pp. 130-33.

7. One method of defence used by the Germans—unusual in colonial warfare at this time—was the extensive laying of landmines. Plenty of dynamite and

blasting gelatine were available, since these explosives were used in peacetime to blast rocks when sinking wells. See Lieutenant-Commander W. Whittall, R.N., *With Botha and Smuts in Africa* (1917), ch. 5.

8. For the Boer Rebellion of 1914, see the *Report on the Outbreak of the Rebellion and Policy of the Government with Regard to its Suppression* (Parliamentary Paper, April 1915, Cd. 7874); *Report of the Judicial Commission of Inquiry into the . . . Rebellion in South Africa* (Cape Town, December 1916); and Sir Charles Lucas, IV, pp. 377-432. The text of the Keimoes Agreement of 17 October, 1914, signed by von Zastrow (for Dr. Seitz) and Maritz, is printed in the *Report of the Judicial Commission of Inquiry . . .* (1916), p. 119.

9. Botha had met the Bastard General Nels van Wyk in March 1915. For a German account of the Bastard rising of 1915, see the official publication *The Treatment of Native and other Populations in the Colonial Possessions of Germany and England* (German Colonial Office, 1919: English translation), pp. 99-105.

10. Volunteers and members of the Reserve were demobilized but permanent members of the Defence Force were interned under their own officers.

11. For the East African campaign, see Charles Hordern and H. Fitz M. Stacke, *Military Operations. East Africa.* Vol. I. August 1914—September 1916 (History of the Great War based on Official Documents, 1941); J. J. O'Sullavan, 'Campaign on German East Africa—Rhodesian Border' (in the *Journal of the African Society*, XV, 1916, pp. 209-15); an article on 'The Campaign in East Africa' (in the *Journal of the Royal United Service Institution*, May 1917); W. Whittall, *With Botha and Smuts in Africa* (1917); Francis Brett Young, *Marching on Tanga* (1917: cheap edition 1940); J. B. Briggs, 'German East Africa during the War' (in the *Journal of the African Society*, April 1917, pp. 196-99); J. H. V. Crowe, *General Smuts' Campaign in East Africa* (1918: introduction by General Smuts); R. V. Dolbey, *Sketches of the East African Campaign* (1918); G. M. Orr, 'Random Recollections of East Africa, 1914-18' (in the *Army Quarterly*, XI, p. 287); C. P. Fendall, *The East African Force, 1915-19* (1921); W. Arning, *Vier Jahre Weltkrieg in Deutsch Ostafrika* (1919); Dr. Ludwig Deppe, *Mit Lettow Vorbeck durch Afrika* (1919); Dr. Heinrich Schnee, *Deutsch Ostafrika im Weltkrieg* (1919); Paul von Lettow Vorbeck, *My Reminiscences of East Africa* (1920); Surgeon E. C. Holtom, R.N., *Two Years' Captivity in German East Africa* (1919); Elspeth Huxley, *White Man's Country. Lord Delamere and the Making of Kenya* (1935), II, chs. 14 and 15; C. J. Thornhill, *Taking Tanganyika* (1937); E. Dane, chs. 5 to 7; H. C. O'Neil, ch. 6; and Sir Charles Lucas, vol. IV, pp. 151-99 (by K. N. Colvile), pp. 297-306 (by Sir Lawrence Wallace), and pp. 459-68 (by K. N. Colvile).

12. See Sir Julian S. Corbett, *Naval Operations*, Vol. II, pp. 236-9, and Vol. III, pp. 63-67; E. Keble Chatterton, *The 'Königsberg' Adventure* (1932); Malcolm Smith, 'The Cruiser in the Swamps' (in *Chambers' Journal*, August, 1936, pp. 584-9); and Max Looff, *Kreuzfahrt und Buschkampf. Mit S.M.S. Königsberg in Deutsch Ost-Afrika* (1927).

13. This river (not to be confused with the upper reaches of the Pangani) forms the upper waters of the River Kingani, which runs into the sea north of Bagamojo.

14. For this phase of the East African campaign see, for example, W. D. Downes, *With the Nigerians in German East Africa* (1919). Captain Downes points

out that the four-day action at Mahina (15-18 October, 1917) 'was one of the biggest engagements ever fought on African soil from the point of view of casualties on both sides. . . . The British lost 2,700 casualties out of a total strength of 4,900 infantry employed' (p. 226).

15. See *Correspondence respecting . . . Operations by Australia against German Possessions in the Western Pacific* (Parliamentary Paper, 1914-16 (Cd. 7975), XLV, 225); *Correspondence relating to the Occupation of German Samoa by . . . New Zealand* (Parliamentary Paper, 1914-16 (Cd. 7972), XLV, 303); L. P. Leary, *New Zealanders in Samoa* (1918); Erich Scheurmann, *Erinnerungen aus der Besetzungszeit Samoas* (1935); and E. Dane, pp. 188-98.

16. See Karl Schultz-Jena, *Der Kampf um Tsingtau* (1918); W. Vollerthun, *Der Kampf um Tsingtau* (1920); G. Plüschon, *My Escape from Donington Hall* (1922: includes account of the siege of Tsingtau); and E. Dane, ch. 10.

Chapter IX

GERMAN COLONIZATION AND THE COLONIAL PROBLEM OF THE 1930's

IN some respects the colonial activities of Germany have been very different from those of Britain, France, Holland and Portugal. The maritime States of Western Europe have been engaged in imperial expansion since the sixteenth and seventeenth centuries. Their overseas empires have played an important part in their political, economic and social development. On the other hand, Germany—like Italy and Belgium—did not acquire overseas possessions until the last quarter of the nineteenth century. The possession of a colonial empire did not have that profound influence upon the national life of modern Germany that it has long had in this country.

If colonies are defined as overseas regions of settlement and commercial exploitation under the political sovereignty of the Mother Country the period of German colonization covers little more than thirty years and is no more than a brief episode in German history. But this is a narrow definition. Settlement, economic exploitation and political sovereignty are important aspects of colonization, but they are not necessarily found together. As Schmitthenner remarks, 'there are colonies which are territorially contiguous with the Mother Country, and there are colonial activities without the flag. Colonization does not emanate from the State alone but from the colonizing activities of the race.' From this point of view the Germans are a colonizing people with centuries of experience. They have traditions of settlement, missionary work and commercial activity which go back far beyond the short-lived colonial empire of 1884-1919.

In the Middle Ages three great movements of German pioneer settlement on the Continent at the expense of various Slav peoples deserve notice; the first to the south-east down the Danube valley, the second in the fertile plains of the Elbe and Oder, and the third along the southern and eastern shores of the Baltic. In all three movements the ambitions of princes and warriors were combined with the more prosaic activities of traders, farmers and missionaries. To these regions of central and eastern Europe the Germans brought a higher culture than they had previously known, and there was considerable development of agriculture, mining and commerce.

The later Middle Ages saw the rise of the Hanseatic League. For a time German shippers and merchants had a large share of the flourishing trade of the North Sea and the Baltic. Hanseatic trading factories in the more remote parts of the Baltic were outposts of German civilization among peoples of comparatively low culture.

From the beginning of the sixteenth century to the end of the eighteenth century, while the maritime Powers of Western Europe were building up great empires overseas, Germany did not play an important part in colonial enterprise. Various factors hindered her development in this respect. The Baltic and North Sea lost much of their old importance when America was discovered and the Cape route to India was opened up. The German ports did not have such easy access to the new trade routes as those of her rivals in the West. Holland, which controlled the Rhine estuary, captured much of the valuable commerce of supplying central Europe with Far Eastern produce. Britain, Holland, France and Spain had powerful national governments which fostered trade and colonial enterprise, but Germany was divided into many virtually independent States. The Holy Roman Empire was too weak to assist German colonization. Numerous domestic problems—the Thirty Years Wars and Austro-Prussian rivalry, for example—kept Germany fully occupied.

Nevertheless Germany's colonial activities were not entirely insignificant in these centuries. Her ships and capital were engaged in Portuguese voyages to the East. Martin Behaim, the Nürnberg globe-maker, travelled under Portuguese patronage. German banking houses, such as the Welsers and Fuggers, shared in the exploitation of Spanish America. The former governed part of Venezuela in 1528-46, and one of their officials (Nikolas Federmann) explored the Bogota plateau. The latter held rights over southern Chile. In the seventeenth century the Great Elector secured for Brandenburg a North Sea port at Emden and tried to found a colonial empire. In 1682 he established an African Commercial Company which sent negro slaves from its Gold Coast stations to St. Thomas in the West Indies. He also set up an East India Company. His successor bought part of the West Indian island of Tobago. But the rivalry of stronger colonial Powers ruined these ventures, and Prussia sold her West African possessions to Holland. She lost interest in enterprises overseas, and neither Frederick the Great nor his successor supported Joachim Nettelbeck's ambitious scheme for the establishment of a Prussian colonial empire. In 1815 Nettelbeck appealed in vain to Gneisenau—a Prussian envoy at the Congress of Vienna— to secure the annexation of a French colony. Austria's attempts at overseas expansion in the eighteenth century also failed. The Austrian East India Company, which sent ships from Ostend (Austrian Netherlands) and Trieste to its trading factories in India, aroused Britain's jealousy and the Emperor Charles VI withdrew from this trade in return for Britain's recognition of Maria Theresa as his heir. Subsequently fresh but abortive attempts were made by the Habsburgs to trade direct with India. In this period, too, there was some German emigration to America, and new settlements were made along the old medieval lines of advance in central and eastern Europe as well as in Russia.

In the years 1815-71 the need for colonies was felt more acutely. Had there been at this time German colonies in the temperate zone many emigrants might have found a new home under their own government instead of settling under foreign flags. Had Germany held tropical possessions she would not have depended upon other countries for her cotton, jute, coffee, tea and cocoa and she would have controlled markets which might have absorbed the manufactures of her growing industries. But Germany still lacked a strong national government. A certain measure of political unity was secured by establishing the Germanic Confederation (1815), and a considerable degree of economic unity was obtained by setting up the Zollverein (1834); but these bodies took little interest in colonial enterprise. There was no national mercantile marine, navy or consular service. Nor did any of the German States attempt to acquire colonies. So it is not surprising that various schemes in the forties for establishing colonial settlements failed. Mexico's offer to sell California to Prussia was not accepted, and no success attended attempts of German companies to found independent settlements in Texas and New Zealand before they were annexed by the U.S.A. and Britain.

Among the writers who promoted a 'colonial consciousness' in Germany at this time were the economists List, Wappäus and Roscher. They argued that the problems raised by the increase in population and the growth of manufactures could be solved by the acquisition of colonies. In *The National System of Political Economy* (1841) Friedrich List wrote that Prussia should adopt a German commercial flag, lay the foundations of a future German fleet, and 'should try whether and how German colonies can be founded in Australia, New Zealand, or in or on other islands of Australasia.' J. E. Wappäus's *Deutsche Auswanderung und Kolonisation* (1846) and Wilhelm Roscher's *Kolonien, Kolonialpolitik und Auswanderung* (1856, Part ii, ch. 4) dealt fully with the problem of German emigration and overseas expansion.

German explorers took a leading part in extending geographical knowledge in this period. Valuable work was done by Barth, von der Decken, Schweinfürth and Nachtigal in Africa, by Alexander von Humboldt, von Spix and von Martius in S. America, by von Richthofen in China, by Leichhardt in Australia, and by von Hochstetter and von Haast in New Zealand. German missionaries were busy in Africa. The Barmen Rhine Mission worked in Namaqualand and the Basel Mission (technically Swiss but run by Germans) on the Gold Coast. Both engaged in trade. German merchants and shippers exploited the commercial resources of the Near East, Africa and the Pacific islands. The Austrian Lloyd of Trieste secured a share of the growing trade of the Eastern Mediterranean. Three Hamburg firms—Hertz, Hansing and O'Swald—built up an extensive trade in E. Africa. The house of Woermann traded in the Cameroons and the house of Godeffroy obtained almost a monopoly of the Samoan copra trade. Hernsheim and Co. were also active in the Pacific. German trade was fostered by the conclusion of commercial treaties. In the fifties the Hansa Towns came to an agreement with the Sultan of Zanzibar, and in the early sixties a Prussian expedition visited southern and eastern Asia to negotiate treaties of commerce.[1]

After the establishment of the German Empire the colonial enthusiasts felt that their day had come. They argued that it was undignified for German explorers, traders and missionaries to work under foreign flags. They deplored the loss to Germany of the emigrants who settled in the U.S.A. and soon adopted the culture of their new homeland. They claimed that a colonial empire would enable Germany to play an effective part in world affairs and that Germany needed new lands for her growing population as well as sources of raw materials and markets for her industries. They observed that economic nationalism was increasing and that Germany herself had adopted a protectionist tariff in 1879. They pointed out that the territories available for colonies were being occupied by other countries and that prompt action was necessary if Germany were not to be left in the cold. Heinrich von Treitschke, in his lectures on Politics at the University of Berlin, declared:

Today we see the nations of Europe busily engaged in creating all over the globe a wholesale aristocracy of the white race. The nation which does not take a share in this great rivalry will play a pitiful part at some later date. It is therefore a vital question for a great nation today to display a craving for colonies.

At first these were the views of a minority. Many Germans had no taste for colonial adventures. There were many domestic problems urgently requiring attention. Colonies would be expensive to acquire—both in money and men—and expansion overseas would antagonize Britain at a time when Germany wanted to isolate France. In Meyer's *Konversations-Lexikon*, a standard work of reference, it was stated that demands for German overseas possessions should be rejected as 'anachronisms and dreams'. 'The aim of every State—and therefore of Germany—is to regulate its internal affairs satisfactorily. Beyond our frontiers we seek nothing save peace and the opportunity to trade as freely as possible.'[2] When in 1880 the Government attempted to underwrite a new company to acquire the Samoan rights of the bankrupt firm of Godeffroy the Reichstag opposition parties, led by Ludwig Bamberger, defeated the project by sixteen votes. Bismarck had no wish for colonies and frequently rejected suggestions that he should place under Imperial protection various overseas settlements and trading posts. And after the colonial empire had been established he still declared: 'Von Haus aus bin ich kein Kolonialmensch.'

But eventually Bismarck did secure colonies for Germany. Various factors influenced his change of policy. The colonial movement was gaining strength and books like Friedrich Fabri's *Does Germany need Colonies?* (1879) and Hübbe-Schleiden's *Deutsche Kolonisation* (1881) were widely read. Several societies to foster colonization flourished in the early eighties. Two of the most important amalgamated as the *Deutsche Kolonialgesellschaft* in 1887. Emigration increased and in 1881-85 amounted to 4.3 per thousand of the population. There were complaints that Germans working overseas suffered from lack of Imperial protection. The expropriation by the British of German settlers in Fiji was a case in point The activities of the British in various parts of Africa, of the French in Tunis, and of the Italians on the shores of the Red Sea heralded a new scramble for colonies.

In 1884 Bismarck placed under Imperial protection Adolf Lüderitz's commercial establishments in the Namaqualand harbour of Angra Pequeña. In six years Germany acquired colonies in Africa (South West and East Africa, the Cameroons and Togoland) and in the Pacific (Kaiser Wilhelmsland in New Guinea and several islands in the Bismarck Archipelago). A few extensions of territory were made after Bismarck's retirement. In 1898 a ninety-nine year lease of the Kiao Chow territory was secured from China. In the following year the Caroline, Pelew and Marianne islands (except Guam) in the Pacific were bought from Spain. In 1900 the Samoan islands of Opulu and Sawaii were acquired and in 1911 part of French Equatorial Africa (the New Cameroons) was obtained in return for the recognition of France's predominant interest in Morocco. In 1914 Germany had a colonial empire of 1,140,000 square miles with an estimated native population of fourteen millions.

The following features of German colonization in 1884-1914 deserve notice. The colonies were acquired rapidly. There was little serious friction with foreign Powers, although Britain and some of self-governing colonies were concerned at the establishment of German rule in regions into which they hoped to expand. Cape Colony was alarmed at the German seizure of South West Africa, and Australia disliked the presence of Germany in New Guinea. But there were Englishmen who agreed with Gladstone when he wished Germany 'Godspeed' in her colonial career and welcomed her as 'our ally in the execution of the great purposes of Providence.' So, although there was some Anglo-German friction and both sides complained of the sharp practices of agents of the other in disputed regions, differences were amicably settled. The peaceful nature of the acquisition of the German colonial empire is in sharp contrast to the history of our own expansion overseas which involved us in long colonial wars in the seventeenth and eighteenth centuries.

There were two elements of weakness in the German colonial empire. First, it had no geographical unity such as that possessed to a considerable degree by the overseas possessions of Britain and France. It was composed of isolated regions which other States had not troubled to occupy. Secondly, it lacked some important strategic points—such as Walfish Bay (South West Africa) and the islands of Zanzibar (off East Africa) and Fernando Po (off the Cameroons)—which were already in the hands of other countries. These weaknesses, combined with lack of command of the sea, made Germany's colonies an easy prey for the Allies during the War.

In all the colonies—except the naval base of Tsingtau (Kiao Chow Bay)—annexation had been preceded by trading. They were tropical plantation and commercial possessions. White settlement was possible only in parts of East and South West Africa. In 1914 the colonial empire contained only 24,000 Germans, many of whom were officials and not permanent residents. At first most of the colonies were ruled by chartered companies. But this system failed and the Imperial Government, somewhat reluctantly, took over colonial administration and left the companies to devote themselves to commercial exploitation. The cost of the colonial empire was considerable. *The Banker* (February, 1937) observed that 'up to 1913

117

her colonial budget deficits cost Germany over a thousand million marks' (£50,000,000). Only Togoland and Samoa were self-supporting. Although the colonies were primarily commercial ventures their trade was not very extensive. In the nineties development was retarded by the policy of Dr. Kayser (Director of the Colonial Section of the Foreign Office, 1890-96) who made unduly large land concessions to a few companies. By 1903 nearly one-third of South West Africa was owned by nine companies. In 1913 the value of the trade of the German colonies was about £13,000,000. Less than half of this (£5,500,000) was with Germany, which was a mere ½ per cent. of the country's total commerce. This was due partly to the poverty of the natural resources of the colonies. But colonial trade was growing steadily.

Germany made many mistakes in governing her colonies. At first the administration was often in the hands of unsuitable officials. A Reichstag deputy complained that 'the colonies are regarded as relief institutions for the benefit of men who have failed at home.' The colonies were governed on Prussian military and bureaucratic lines which proved to be unsatisfactory. Natives frequently lost their land; they were liable to perform unpaid forced labour; they were often cruelly treated. Little attention was paid to their old-established customs. Among high colonial officials who were dismissed for atrocious cruelty were Carl Peters, Wehlan, von Horn, von Leist, and von Puttkamer. Readers of *A Footnote to History* (1892) will recall Robert Louis Stevenson's indictment of German colonial methods in Samoa in the eighties. Misgovernment led to risings in several colonies and they were savagely suppressed. General Trotha, the commander in South West Africa, declared: 'The Hereros must leave the land. If they refuse I shall compel them with the gun. I shall assume charge of no more women and children, but shall drive them back to their people or let them be shot at.' The wretched natives were driven into the desert and some 14,000 perished.

But there is a brighter side of German colonial administration. The Arab slave trade was suppressed in East Africa with British co-operation. Many officials, teachers, missionaries and doctors did good work and showed a sympathetic understanding of the natives. Von Wissmann, Dr. Solf and Dr. Schnee were admirable administrators. Among medical men Dr. Koch deserves mention for his researches into sleeping-sickness. Many tributes were paid before the War by foreign observers to Germany's good work in her colonies. Selections were printed by W. H. Solf in *Germany's Right to Recover her Colonies* (1919) and by A. Mansfeld and G. Hildebrand in *Englische Urteile über die deutsche Kolonialarbeit* (1919).

There was an improvement in German colonial administration after the exposure in 1906 by Social Democrats, Progressives and the Catholic Centre Party of 'colonial scandals'. Dr. Dernburg, Colonial Secretary in 1907-1910, inaugurated the new policy. Officials were carefully trained at the Hamburg Colonial Institute. The Government gradually bought back land from the colonial companies. Forced labour was restricted, and arrangements were made to abolish domestic slavery. Public works were undertaken. The railway from Dar-es-Salaam to Kigoma (on Lake Tanganyika) was completed in 1914. But the new colonial policy had been in force for only eight years when war broke out in 1914 so that its achievements were limited.

Germany tried to extend her colonial empire before the first World War. 'We do not want to put anyone in the shade,' declared Prince von Bülow in 1897, 'but we demand for ourselves a place in the sun.' Rivalry with France over Morocco nearly precipitated war in 1911. She secured economic privileges in the Chinese province of Shantung and in the Ottoman Empire where she was building the Baghdad Railway. Agreements in 1898 and 1913 foreshadowed a possible Anglo-German partition of Portugal's African colonies. During the first World War colonial enthusiasts hoped to extend the overseas empire. They demanded the establishment of a German 'Mittel-Afrika', the linking together of existing colonies at the expense of Allied possessions. Had Germany ever been in a position to dictate peace the Allies would have suffered severe colonial losses. When Russia and Rumania were defeated Germany showed no mercy. The German colonies, however, were easily conquered. Only in East Africa did the Germans put up serious resistance. In 1914, since she had few troops in Africa, Germany tried to prevent hostilities from spreading to her possessions in the Congo basin which were— by Article 11 of the Berlin Congo Act (1885)—to be, if possible, 'under the rule of neutrality' in wartime. She failed. Each side accused the other of attacking first in Africa.[3]

In 1919 the victors partitioned the German colonial empire largely on the basis of Allied agreements made during the war. Much German private property in the colonies was confiscated. There was no 'free, open-minded and absolutely impartial adjustment of all colonial claims' such as was contemplated by the fifth of Wilson's Fourteen Points. The colonies were held as 'mandates' from the League of Nations. The mandatory Powers tried to assimilate the former German colonies to their own possessions as far as possible. These attempts did not always succeed. By 1938 South West Africa had not become a fifth province of the Union of South Africa and

Tanganyika (German East Africa) had not been absorbed in a federation of British East African possessions. The number of Germans living in the former colonies declined to some 16,000 (1938). In 1914 in South West Africa 84 per cent. of the whites were Germans: in 1926 only 37 per cent. Germany's share in the commerce of these regions had declined. Half of the goods bought by East Africa in 1912 came from Germany, but in 1935 the percentage was only 10.7.

After the first World War there was a vigorous propaganda by various German societies—federated after 1933 in the *Reichs-kolonialbund*—in favour of the return of the colonies. But not all Germans agreed that colonial enterprise was desirable. It is interesting to find in Adolf Hitler's *Mein Kampf* (1925-27) a condemnation of the 'foolish colonial policy' of the pre-war era. The National Socialists, he wrote, would 'definitely break with the pre-war colonial and commercial policy and adopt the "land-policy" of the future'. This new policy would be to conquer in the east—mainly at Russia's expense—new lands suitable for large-scale German agricultural settlement. After *Mein Kampf* was written, however, Hitler frequently demanded the return of former German colonies.

The following arguments were used to justify the claim for the revival of Germany's overseas empire. The reasons given by the Allies for depriving Germany of her colonial possessions were severely criticized. Germans stigmatized as the 'colonial guilt lie' (*Kolonialschuldlüge*) the charges of colonial maladministration brought against them during the first World War. They said that when natives were ill-treated the responsible officials were punished. Germans claimed that they never militarized the natives they controlled whereas other countries, such as France, did so. They considered that their colonial record was better than that of Belgium or Portugal and would stand comparison with that of Britain or France. They pointed to the good work of missionaries and teachers and to the contributions to geographical, agricultural, anthropological and medical knowledge made by Germans in their colonies. Germany demanded 'equality of status' (*Gleichberechtigung*) with other Great Powers and wanted equality in colonial matters. It was regarded as unfair that several European States should have vast colonial possessions while Germany had none. According to the *Economist* (26 October, 1935) the British Empire alone had over half of the world's production of gold, nickel, wool, jute, rubber and cocoa; over 30 per cent. of that of zinc, lead and tin; and 20 per cent. of that of copra, cotton, copper, coal and silver. Germany, with 370 persons to the square mile, was alleged to be 'overpopulated'—

Volk ohne Raum was a popular slogan—and colonies might absorb German settlers. Colonies would provide Germany with raw materials and buy German manufactured goods. She could not obtain enough foreign currency for overseas trade. No such difficulty would arise when commodities were exchanged between areas using the same money. Germans criticized the use of pre-war trade figures to prove that the colonies were of little economic value. Germany possessed colonies for only thirty years, and there was no time for greater economic progress than was actually achieved. Before 1933 it was urged that the democratic Germany of the Weimar régime would not repeat the errors of pre-war governments and was peculiarly well fitted to rule native peoples. This argument was no longer valid in the period of Nazi rule.

Those who opposed the revival of the German colonial empire argued on these lines. They agreed that many of the charges brought during the first World War against the Germans as colonizers could not be sustained and that it had been impolitic to partition their overseas possessions. But it was said to be impracticable to rectify the mistakes of the Treaty of Versailles by returning Germany's colonies in the 1930's. These possessions had been in other hands for some twenty years, and the new rulers had invested large sums in them and had sent officials, missionaries and settlers who were doing excellent work there. Temporary, but serious, dislocation might follow if the colonies were returned. It was said that many economists were agreed that Germany would derive little economic benefit from her former possessions. Her former colonies produced hardly any of the six raw materials which Goebbels considered essential to a powerful State—coal, iron, oil, cotton, rubber and copper. The Royal Institute of International Affairs's pamphlet on *Raw Materials and Colonies* (1936) commented upon 'the negligible significance of the resources of the mandated territories, apart from South West Africa's vanadium, Tanganyika's sisal, Nauru's phosphates . . .' It was observed that numerous countries—such as Poland and Czecho-Slovakia—were reasonably prosperous without colonies. Germany admittedly could not get certain raw materials, but this was said to be due not to lack of colonies but to lack of money. If Germany chose to spend £1,000,000,000 per annum upon armaments rather than upon raw materials for the consumption goods industry that was her affair. To the German argument that her former colonies would absorb some of her 'surplus population' it was answered first, that the colonies were not suited to large-scale white settlement and secondly, that there was little likelihood of a permanent increase in Germany's population. Rosenberg spoke of

121

'Germany's future 150 million inhabitants,' but it was doubtful if half this total would ever be reached, and it seemed probable that the population of Germany (within her frontiers of that time) would begin to decline before the middle of the twentieth century. Doubts were expressed whether Hitler's Government, with its unusual views on 'Aryan' and 'non-Aryan' races, was well suited to rule backward 'non-Aryan' peoples. It was alleged that Germany would not be satisfied with her former colonies. She had tried to expand her empire before the first World War and might attempt to do so again. Should she establish overseas military, naval and air establishments Britain would have had to undertake costly defensive measures. Moreover, even if Britain had favoured the return of German colonies, it would probably have been impossible to induce South Africa, Australia and New Zealand to surrender their mandates, not to speak of France. Japan appeared to be friendly with Germany but there can be little doubt what her answer would be if Germany had demanded the return of the islands she once owned in the Northern Pacific.

REFERENCES

1. P. E. Schramm, *Deutschland und Ubersee* (1950).
2. Meyer's *Konversations-Lexikon*, 3rd edn., Vol. X (1877): article on colonies·
3. G. K. Johannsen and H. H. Kraft state in their book on *Germany's Colonial Problem* (1937) that 'under the Congo Act of 1885 . . . the colonies of the European Powers in Central Africa were declared to be neutral. This provision of International Law was infringed by her enemies in the War when they initiated warlike actions against Germany's East African colony on August 5, 1914' (p. 19). This opinion appears to have been widely held in Germany and was inaccurate. General von Lettow-Vorbeck, the able German commander in E. Africa, stated correctly in *My Reminiscences of East Africa*: 'The Congo Act . . . only says that in case of conflict between two of the Powers concerned, a third Power may offer its good services as mediator. But as far as I know this step was not taken by any Power' (p. 19).

BIBLIOGRAPHICAL NOTE

Chapter I

BIBLIOGRAPHY. Dahlmann-Waitz, *Quellenkunde der deutschen Geschichte* (9th edn., 1931), p. 267.

DOCUMENTS. The diplomatic negotiations concerning the acquisition of German colonies may be studied in documents printed in *Die Grosse Politik der europäischen Kabinette 1871-1914*. Selections from these documents are contained in E. T. S. Dugdale, *German Diplomatic Documents* (4 vols., 1928-31); see also the English and French documents on the origin of the Great War. Less reliable but not without interest are the documents printed in the *Parliamentary Papers* (*e.g.* 1884-85, LIV-LVI; 1885, LVI; 1887, LXI; 1888, LXXIV; 1889, LVI; 1890, LI; 1894, XCVI; 1900, CV). The publications of the colonial section of the German Foreign Office and of the German Colonial Office also deserve study.

PERIODICALS. *Deutsche Kolonialzeitung* (1884-1922); *Deutsches Kolonialblatt* (1890-1921).

GENERAL WORKS. P. E. Schramm, *Deutschland und Übersee* (1950); Paul Leutwein (editor), *Dreissig Jahre Deutsches Kolonialpolitik* (*c.* 1914); Hans Meyer (editor), *Das Deutsche Kolonialreich* (2 vols., 1909-10); Heinrich Schnee (editor), *Deutsches Kolonial Lexikon* (3 vols., 1920); André Chéradame, *La colonisation et les colonies allemandes* (1905); Alfred Zimmermann, *Geschichte der deutschen Kolonialpolitik* (1914); Mary Evelyn Townsend, *The Rise and Fall of Germany's Colonial Empire 1884-1914* (1930); P. Decharme, *Compagnies et sociétés coloniales allemandes* (1903); Jäckel, *Die Landgesellschaften in den deutschen Schutzgebieten* (1909); Evans Lewin, *The Germans and Africa* (1915); W. Gothard, *Germany's Colonial Work in Africa* (Bielefeld, 1931).

SPECIAL TOPICS: **Acquisition of colonies.** T. Sommerlad, *Der deutsche Kolonialgedanke und sein Werden im 19en Jahrhundert* (1918); M. E. Townsend, *Origins of Modern German Colonialism 1871-85* (1921); M. von Hagen, *Bismarck's Kolonialpolitik* (1923); E. Brandenburg, *From Bismarck to the World War: a History of*

123

German Foreign Policy 1870-1914 (1927); W. L. Langer, *European Alliances and Alignments 1871-90* (1931).

Development of separate colonies. *Nachrichten über Kaiser Wilhelmsland und das Bismarckarchipel* (1885-98); H. Schinz, *Deutsch Ostafrika* . . . (1906); H. Weicher, *Kiautschau* . . . (1908); L. Sander, *Geschichte der deutschen Kolonialgesellschaft in Süd-West Afrika* . . . (2 vols., 1912); H. Vedder, *Das alte Südwestafrika* (1934).

Native Risings. *Die Kämpfe der deutschen Truppen in Süd-West Afrika* (official account by German General Staff, 2 vols., 1906-7); R. Schmidt, *Geschichte des Araberaufstandes in Ostafrika* ... (1892); A. von Götzen, *Deutsch-Ostafrika im Aufstand 1905-6* (1909); R. M. Bell, 'The Maji-Maji Rebellion in the Liwale District' (*Tanganyika Notes and Records*, No. 28, January 1950).

Economic conditions. B. Dernburg, *Die deutschen Kapitalinteressen in den deutschen Schutzgebieten* (1907); A. F. Calvert, *German East Africa* (1917).

Chapter II

Origins of modern German Colonization. Mary Evelyn Townsend, *Origins of Modern German Colonialism 1871-85* (1921); M. Hansen, *German Schemes of Colonisation before 1860* (1924); T. Somerlad, *Der deutsche Kolonialgedanke und sein Werden im 19 Jahrhundert* (1918); Percy Ernst Schramm, *Deutschland und Übersee* (1950); Richard Schück, *Brandenburg-Preussens Kolonialpolitik* . . . *1647-1721* (2 vols.); M. Coppius, *Hamburgs Bedeutung auf dem Gebiet der deutschen Kolonialpolitik* (1905); Otto Mathies, *Hamburgs Reederei 1814-1914* (1924); Karl Brackmann, *Fünfzig Jahre deutscher Afrikaschiffahrt* (1935); R. Hertz, *Das Hamburger Seehandelshaus J. C. Godeffroy & Sohn* (1922); Ernst Hieke, *Zur Geschichte des deutschen Handels mit Ostafrika. Das Hamburgische Handelshaus Wm. O'Swald & Co.*, Vol. I, 1830-70 (1939); Ernst Hieke, 'Das hamburgische Handelshaus Wm. O'Swald & Co. und der Beginn des deutschen Afrikahandels 1848-53' (*Vierteljahrschrift für Sozial- und Wirtschafts-Geschichte*, Vol. XXX, 1937, pp. 347-374).

Bismarck's Colonial Policy. Dr. Charpentier, *Entwicklungsgeschichte der Kolonialpolitik des deutschen Reiches* (1886); W. Weissborn, *Sechs Jahre deutscher Colonialpolitik* (1890); Oscar Cannstatt, *Fürst Bismarcks kolonialpolitisches Initiative* (1908); Kurt

BIBLIOGRAPHICAL NOTE

Herrfurth, Fürst Bismarck und die Kolonialpolitik (1917); Maximilian von Hagen, *Bismarcks Kolonialpolitik* (1923); Walther Stuhlmacher, *Bismarcks Kolonialpolitik* (1917); W. O. Aydelotte, *Bismarck and British Colonial Policy* (1937); A. J. P. Taylor, *Germany's first Bid for Colonies, 1884-5* (1938); E. Eyck, *Bismarck* (3 vols., 1941-4), pp. 394-425.

Bismarck and the West Africa (Congo) Conference. Howard E. Yarnall, *The Great Powers and the Congo Conference* . . . (University of Göttingen dissertation, 1934); S. E. Crowe, *The Berlin West Africa Conference* (1942).

German East Africa. J. Wagner, *Deutsch Ostafrika. Geschichte der Gesellschaft für deutsche Kolonisation und die deutsche Ostafrikanische Gesellschaft* (1886); Carl Peters, *Das Deutsch-Ostafrikanische Schutzgebiet* (1895); Carl Peters, *Die Gründung von Deutsch-Ostafrika* (1906); Joachim von Pfeil, *Die Erwerbung von Deutsch-Ostafrika* (new edition, 1907); Rochus Schmidt, *Geschichte des Araberaufstandes in Ost-Afrika* (1892); Eugéne Plumon, *La colonie allemande de l'Afrique orientale* . . . (University of Rennes dissertation, 1905); Most, 'Die wirtschaftliche Entwicklung Deutsch-Ostafrika, 1885-1905' (*Jahresbericht der . Klosterschule Rossleben, 1906*, pp. 3-28); Hermann Paasche, *Deutsch-Ostafrika: wirtschaftliche Studien* (1906); A. Rousse, *Zwanzig Jahre Ansieder in Deutsch Ost-Afrika* (1929).

South West Africa. Amelia Lawrence Hodge, *Angra Pequeña* (University of Munich dissertation 1936); H. Vedder, *Das alte Südwestafrika* (1934); L. Sander, *Geschichte der deutschen Kolonialgesellschaft fur Südwestafrika* (2 vols., 1912); Wilhelm Schüssler, *Adolf Lüderitz* . . . (1936); Brugge and Fowler, *Kurze Übersicht über die Tätigkeit der deutschen Colonial-Gesellschaft fur Südwestafrika* (1907).

The Cameroons. H. R. Rudin, *Germans in the Cameroons, 1884-1914* (1938).

The Pacific. *Nachrichten uber Kaiser Wilhelms Land und den Bismarckarchipel* (3 vols., 1875-80: issued by the New Guinea Company); Sylvia Masterman, *The Origins of International Rivalry in the Pacific, 1845-84* (1934); Robert Louis Stevenson, *A Footnote to History* (1892); William Churchill, 'Germany's lost Pacific Empire' (*Geographical Review*, Vol. X, 1920, pp. 84-90).

125

Economic Development. *Wirtschaftsatlas der deutschen Kolonien* (Berlin, 1906); Otto Mayer, *Die Entwicklung der Handelsbeziehungen Deutschlands zu seinen Kolonien* (1913); M. Schanz, *Cotton Growing in German Colonies* (Manchester, 1910).

Native Welfare. K. Weyle, *Native Life in East Africa* (1909); D. Carl Mirbt, *Mission und Kolonialpolitik in den deutschen Schutzgebieten* (1910); Martin Schlunk, *Das Schulwesen in den deutschen Schutzgebieten* (1914).

Chapter III

Works on the German colonies in which discussions will be found relating to their economic development include the following: William Harbutt Dawson, *The Evolution of Modern Germany* (1911 edition), chaps. 13 and 14 ; and *Germany under the Treaty* (1933), chap. 12. General works on colonies, which include accounts of German colonization, are: Norman Angell, *This Have and Have-Not Business* (1936), and Grover Clark, *A Place in the Sun* (1936). The case for the return of the German colonies after the first World War may be studied in Heinrich Schnee, *German Colonisation Past and Future* (1926), and G. Kurt Johannsen and H. H. Kraft, *Germany's Colonial Problem* (1937): the case against in a report of the Empire Economic Union entitled *The British Colonial Empire and the German Claim* (1937).

Chapters IV and V

See Rudolf Hermann, *Die Handelsbeziehungen Deutschlands zu seinen Schutzgebieten* (Berlin, 1899); André Chéradame, *La colonisation et les colonies allemandes* (Paris, 1905: includes useful statistical tables); A. Seidel, *Der gegenwärtige Handel der deutschen Schutzgebiete und die Mittel zu seiner Ausdehnung* (Giessen, 1907); Bernhard Dernburg, *Zielpunkte des deutschen Kolonialwesens* (two lectures; Berlin, 1907); Moritz J. Bonn, *Nationale Kolonialpolitik* (Munich, 1910) and *Die Neugestaltung unserer kolonialen Aufgaben* (Tübingen, 1911); Otto Jöhlinger, *Die wirtschaftliche Bedeutung unserer Kolonien* (Berlin, 1910); C. G. Barth, *Unsere Schutzgebiete nach ihren wirtschaftlichen Verhältnissen* (Leipzig, 1910); Otto Mayer, *Die Entwicklung der Handelsbeziehungen Deutschlands zu seinen Kolonien* (Munich, 1913: includes useful statistical tables); Alfred Zimmermann, *Geschichte der deutschen Kolonialpolitik* (Berlin, 1914); Heinrich Schnee (editor), *Deutsches Kolonial-Lexikon*

(3 vols., Leipzig, 1920); A. Sartorius von Waltershausen, *Deutsche Wirtschaftsgeschichte 1815-1914* (second edition, Jena, 1923), pp. 358-73; Ludwig Schön, *Das koloniale Deutschland* (articles reprinted from the Berlin *Börsen-Zeitung*, 1937). Cf. *Wirtschaftsatlas der deutschen Kolonien* (Berlin, 1906).

Chapter VI

See R. Menz, *Deutsche Arbeit in Kleinasien* (Berlin, 1893); N. Verney and G. Dambmann, *Les puissances étrangères dans le Levant* (Paris, 1900); V. Chirol, *The Middle Eastern Question* (1903); Angus Hamilton, *Problems of the Middle East* (1909); H. Grothe, *Die asiatische Türkei und die deutschen Interessen* (Halle a/S, 1913); K. Helfferich, *Die deutsche Türkenpolitik* (Berlin, 1921); M. Moukhtar, *La Turkie, l'Allemagne et l'Europe* ... (Paris, 1924); H. Holborn, *Deutschland und die Türkei* (Berlin, 1928); H. Hoskins, *British Routes to India* (Philadelphia, 1928); Hans Kohn, *Die Europäisierung des Orients* (Berlin, 1934); A. Raab, *Die Politik Deutschlands im nahen Orient 1878-1907* (Vienna, 1936) and B. G. Martin, *German-Persian Diplomatic Relations, 1873-1912* (1959). There is much useful statistical information in the *Levante-Handbuch* (3rd ed.; Berlin, 1914), edited by Davis Trietsche.

Chapter VII

See Heinrich Schnee, *Deutschostafrika im Weltkrieg* (Leipzig, 1919), chs. 8-11, 15, 18, 19, 22, and General Paul von Lettow Vorbeck, *My Reminiscences of East Africa* (1920), Part I, chs. 1, 5, 7, 8, and Part II, ch. 8. For economic conditions on the eve of the war see the article 'Deutsch Ostafrika' in the *Deutsches Kolonial-Lexikon* (3 vols., ed. by H. Schnee), I, 357-405 and Otto Mayer, *Die Entwicklung der Handelsbeziehungen Deutschlands zu seinen Kolonien* (1913), pp. 47-69 and 113-29.

Chapter VIII

See G. M. Wrigley, 'The Military Campaigns against Germany's African Colonies' (in the *Geographical Review*, published by the American Geographical Society, vol. V, January-June, 1918, pp. 44-65: includes useful list of contemporary reports, books and articles); H. C. O'Neil, *The War in Africa and the Far East* (1918); E. Dane, *British Campaigns in Africa and the Pacific, 1914-18* (1919); Sir Charles Lucas, *The Empire at War*, vol. IV (1924). For details of British forces employed and casualties in South West and

East Africa, see *Statistics of the Military Effort of the British Empire during the Great War, 1914-20* (H.M. Stationery Office, 1922).

Chapter IX

Thoe Sommerlad, *Der deutsche Kolonialgedanke und sein Werden im 19. Jahrhundert* (Halle an der Saale, 1918); M. Hansen, *German Schemes of Colonization before 1860* (*Smith College Studies in History*, Vol. IX, 1924); Max von Koschitzky, *Deutsche Colonialgeschichte* (two parts in one volume, Leipzig, 1920); Walter Stuhlmacher, *Bismarcks Kolonialpolitik* (Halle an der Saale, 1927, based on German official documents printed in *Die Grosse Politik*); Lionel Birch, *The Demand for Colonies* (London, 1936); Hans Grimm, *Volk ohne Raum* (Munich, 1926. Cheap edition, 1931).

APPENDIX A

TABLE 1

The initial expenses incurred by the New Guinea Company in establishing an administration (to December 1886) were as follows:

	Marks
Purchase of seven ships	818,500
Equipment for seven ships	110,900
Salaries of Company's officials	328,570
Provisions for trading stations imported from Europe	108,100
Houses and furniture	180,700
Equipment for trading stations imported from Europe and Australia	156,150
	1,702,920

See Kurt Herrfurth, *Fürst Bismarck und die Kolonialpolitik*, (1917), p. 173.

TABLE 2

Estimated initial expenses of the Jaluit Company (1888)

	Marks
Purchase of land and erection of landing stages	10,000
House and furniture for Governor and Secretary	10,000
House and furniture for six policemen	7,000
Cutter (70 to 80 tons)	50,000
Provisions and weapons	8,000
Miscellaneous	5,000
	90,000

See Kurt Herrfurth, *Fürst Bismarck und die Kolonialpolitik*, (1917), p. 175.

TABLE 3

Estimated annual expenditure of Jaluit Company

	Marks
Governor's salary	20,000
Secretary's salary	10,000
Wages of six policemen	5,000
Uniforms and provisions for six policemen	2,000
Cost of running cutter	30,000
Miscellaneous	3,000
	70,000

See K. Herrfurth, op. cit., p. 175.

TABLE 4

Budget of the Marshall Islands

	Total Expenditure	Revenue raised locally
	Marks	Marks
1899	640,000	80,000
1900	900,000	90,000
1901	860,000	100,000
1902	1,100,000	80,000
1903	1,050,000	130,000
1904	1,070,000	140,000

See Alfred Zimmermann, *Geschichte der deutschen Kolonialpolitik*, (1914), p. 283.

TABLE 5

German Colonies	Area (sq. miles)	Administration after 1919

AFRICA

East Africa — 384,000
1. Tanganyika Territory: British mandate
2. Ruanda and Urundi districts: Belgian mandate
3. Kionga district (mouth of River Rovuma): Portuguese mandate

South West Africa — 322,000
1. Union of South Africa mandate
2. Caprivizipfel (the 'corridor' to the Zambezi) administered under Bechuanaland Protectorate

Cameroons (Kamerun) 305,000
1. New Cameroons ('corridors' to River Congo and Ubangi ceded by France to Germany in 1911) returned to France: no mandate
2. Remainder held as mandates by France (166,000 sq. miles) and Britain (34,200 sq. miles)

Togoland — 34,000
Divided between Britain and France (mandates)

PACIFIC OCEAN AND CHINA

Caroline, Marianne and Marshall Islands — 1,000
Japanese mandate

New Guinea and Bismarck Archipelago — 93,000
Commonwealth of Australia mandate. Nauru Island was a British Empire mandate: governed by Britain, Australia and New Zealand: administration changed every five years

Samoa (Opolu and Sawaii) — 1,000
New Zealand mandate

Kiao Chow — 200
Conquered from Germany by Japan and ceded to China.

TABLE 6

Distribution of the White Population in Germany's Colonies in Africa and the Pacific (excluding Kiao Chow), 1911

	Civil Servants	Army and Police	Mission-aries and Clergy	Mer-chants, Shop-keepers, Innkeepers	Artisans, Labourers Miners	Planters and Farmers	Other Male Inhabi-tants	Women and Children	Total White Popu-lation	Total German Popu-lation
South West Africa	881	2,072	70	1,035	2,572	1,390	895	5,047	13,962	11,140
East Africa	401	195	428	311	293	683	538	1,378	4,227	3,113
Cameroons	244	119	117	436	84	111	122	222	1,455	1,311
Togoland	87	—	66	64	29	5	50	62	363	327
Pacific colonies	121	—	266	288	98	208	140	539	1,660	1,056
Totals	1,734	2,386	947	2,134	3,076	2,397	1,745	7,248	21,667	16,947

132

TABLE 7

Foreign Trade of the German Colonies, 1901-1912 (in thousands of Marks)*

	Four African Colonies		Colonies in the Pacific		Kiao Chow		Total Trade		Excess of Imports over Exports
	Imports	Exports	Imports	Exports	Imports	Exports	Imports	Exports	
1901	33,406	15,820	4,450	3,568	13,459	5,289	51,615	24,677	26,938
1902	37,024	18,342	5,879	3,776	25,645	8,909	68,548	31,027	37,558
1903	34,862	21,678	6,946	3,885	34,974	14,749	76,782	40,312	36,470
1904	40,672	20,821	5,796	4,002	44,870	19,983	91,338	44,806	46,532
1905	62,514	23,438	8,858	4,398	69,176	24,717	140,548	52,553	87,995
1906	113,517	25,523	8,381	5,641	82,374	34,225	204,272	65,389	138,883
1907	80,199	35,923	8,546	5,240	55,380	32,597	144,125	73,760	70,365
1908	84,264	37,726	7,593	8,724	69,041	47,344	160,898	93,794	67,104
1909	97,613	58,264	9,799	11,350	65,464	54,732	172,876	124,346	48,530
1910	119,949	82,643	9,708	18,199	69,375	60,561	199,032	161,403	37,629
1911	130,131	81,579	12,081	16,416	114,938	80,295	257,150	178,290	78,860
1912	128,478	103,748	14,201	17,132	121,254	79,640	263,933	200,520	63,415

*This table is based on tables in the *Deutsches Kolonial-Lexikon*, II, p. 34, and André Touzet, *Le Problème Colonial et la Paix du Monde*. *Les Revendications Coloniales Allemandes* (1937), p. 228. The figures include the import and export of money except for Samoa. The sharp rise in the imports of the African colonies in 1906 is due to the fact that Government goods sent to South West Africa were included in that year, but were excluded in 1904-5 (Herero rebellion). The Togoland statistics include the value of the duties levied upon imports before 1905 but not afterwards. The Kiao Chow figures are reckoned from 1 October to 30 September. Until the end of 1905 they represent the transit trade of the free port. They include that part of the trade of the Chinese province of Shantung which passed through Kiao Chow.

TABLE 8

Table illustrating the extent to which the Colonies supplied Germany with raw materials and other products (as percentage of Germany's total consumption in 1910)

	Quantity (per cent.)	Value (per cent.)
Cotton	0·25	0·25
Rubber	13·62	12·33
Oils and fats	2·12	2·66
Tropical timber	4·07	3·43
Wool	0·03	0·02
Hides and skins	0·15	0·17
Wax	8·09	8·14
Ivory	6·06	6·09
Mica	6·21	6·31
Precious stones	0·30	37·35

See Otto Mayer, *Die Entwicklung der Handelsbeziehungen Deutschlands zu seinen Kolonien* (1913), p. 178.

TABLE 9

Germany's Commercial Relations with her Colonies from 1891 to 1910 in Relation to her Total Trade (in million marks)

	IMPORTS			EXPORTS		
	Total Imports to Germany	Imports from the Colonies	Percent-age of Colonial Imports	Total Exports from Germany	Exports to the Colonies	Percent-age of Exports to Colonies
1891	4,656,0	5,9	0·13	3,503,9	6,0	0·17
1892	4,435,5	4,4	0·10	3,346,1	5,3	0·16
1893	4,306,4	4,2	0·10	3,397,2	4,8	0·14
1894	4,632,8	3,8	0·08	3,141,5	4,6	0·15
1895	4,371,5	3,3	0·08	3,530,3	4,5	0·13
1896	4,808,8	4,3	0·09	3,982,5	5,5	0·14
1897	5,048,5	4,6	0·09	3,937,5	8,6	0·22
1898	5,798,7	4,6	0·07	4,264,6	10,9	0·25
1899	6,084,1	4,8	0·07	4,529,8	14,7	0·32
1900	6,320,4	6,5	0·10	4,893,8	23,3	0·48
1901	5,710,3	5,8	0·10	4,512,6	20,7	0·46
1902	5,805,8	6,9	0·12	4,812,8	21,1	0·44
1903	6,321,1	7,3	0·12	5,130,3	23,5	0·46
1904	6,854,5	11,1	0·16	5,315,6	33,1	0·62
1905	7,436,3	17,7	0·24	5,841,8	43,6	0·74
1906	8,438,6	20,3	0·24	6,475,6	43,0	0·67
1907	9,003,3	22,9	0·25	7,094,9	37,9	0·53
1908	8,077,1	21,9	0·27	6,481,5	36,5	0·56
1909	8,860,4	29,4	0·33	6,858,7	41,8	0·61
1910	9,310,0	50,1	0·54	7,644,2	55,6	0·73

See last table in Otto Mayer, *Die Entwicklung der Handelsbeziehungen Deutschlands zu seinen Kolonien* (1913).

TABLE 10

German Trade with the Middle East, 1908-13

	In million marks					
	1908	1909	1910	1911	1912	1913
Imports from:						
Turkey	47·56	57·29	67·45	70·09	77·65	73·93
Egypt	38·37	51·50	64·10	64·70	80·63	—
Persia	0·20	0·32	0·79	1·11	—	—
Exports to:						
Turkey	64·07	78.92	104·87	112·88	112·84	98·42
Egypt	23·22	23·43	26·19	31·15	27·29	—
Persia	—	0·12	0·46	0·22	0·14	0·15

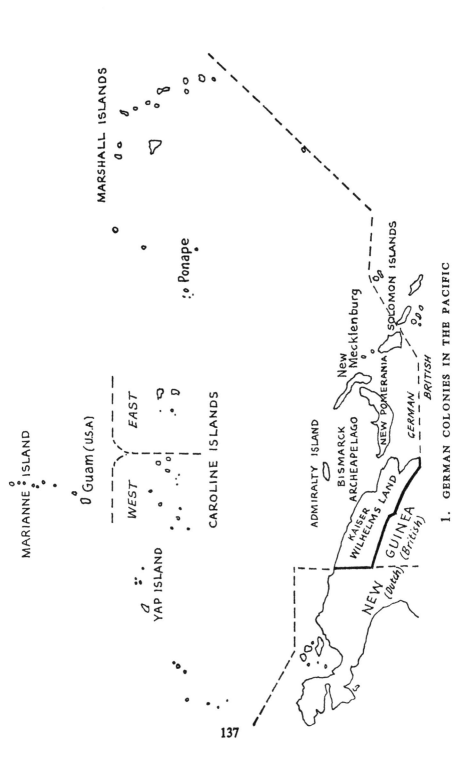

1. GERMAN COLONIES IN THE PACIFIC

MARSHALL ISLANDS

MARIANNE ISLAND

Guam (U.S.A)

Ponape

YAP ISLAND

WEST   EAST

CAROLINE ISLANDS

ADMIRALTY ISLAND

BISMARCK ARCHEAPELAGO

New Mecklenburg

NEW POMERANIA

SOLOMON ISLANDS

KAISER WILHELMS LAND

GERMAN

BRITISH

NEW GUINEA
(Dutch) (British)

137

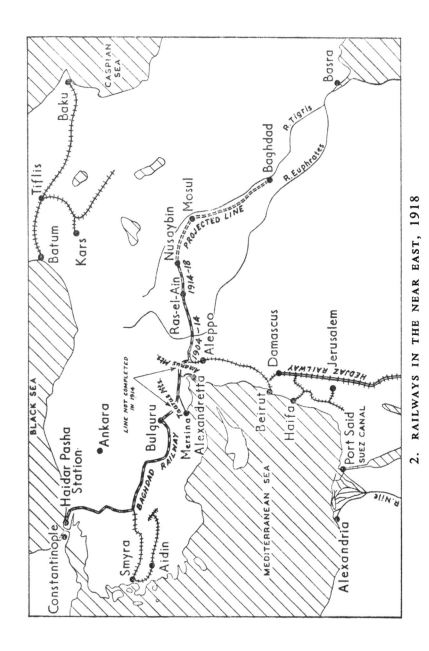

2. RAILWAYS IN THE NEAR EAST, 1918

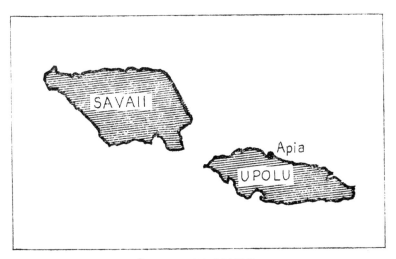

3. GERMAN SAMAO

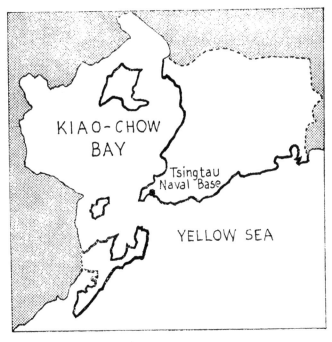

4. KIAO CHOW

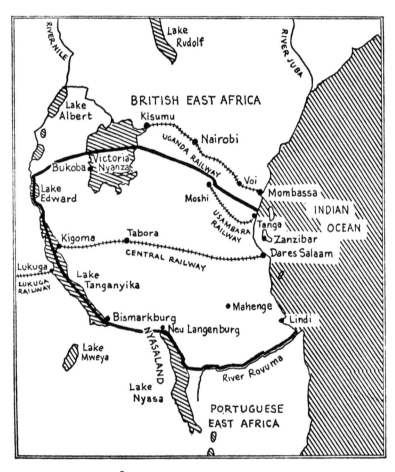

5. GERMAN EAST AFRICA

TOGOLAND

CAMEROONS

GULF OF
GUINEA

Victoria
Nyanza

INDIAN
OCEAN

Lake
Tanganyika

GERMAN
EAST
AFRICA

Pemba
ZANZIBAR
(British)

ATLANTIC

OCEAN

Lake
Nyasa

S.W.
AFRICA Caprivizipfel

WALFISH BAY
(British)

RED SEA

...... Frontiers of the Cameroons to 1911

6. GERMAN COLONIES IN AFRICA

141

INDEX